THE IMPOSTER SYNDROME

How to Stop Feeling like a Fraud at Work, Build Your
Confidence and Stop the Inner Critic

PHIL ROBERTS

Contents

Introduction   v

1. WHAT IMPOSTER SYNDROME IS   1
   Characteristics of IS   2
   Clance IP Test   4
   What Causes IS?   6
   Common Types of IS   11
   Chapter Summary   13

2. HOW TO OVERCOME ANALYSIS -   15
   PARALYSIS
   Steps to Overcome Perfectionism   16
   Perfectionist thinking   19
   Chapter Summary   29

3. IMPOSTER WORKAHOLICS   31
   How to Find Validation From Within   36
   Chapter Summary   46

4. WHEN TRYING HARD BECOMES   47
   TOO MUCH
   Growing Up Feeling Not Good Enough   49
   Listening to & Understanding Your Fear of   51
   Not Being Good Enough
   How to Feel Good Enough About Yourself   53
   Surrender to Not Knowing Everything   55
   Chapter Summary   58

5. WHEN YOU DON'T SUCCEED ON YOUR   59
   FIRST TRY
   How Natural Geniuses Hold Themselves Back   60
   Misconceptions Surrounding Natural Geniuses   67
   Admit You Don't Know It All & Embrace   68
   Learning
   Chapter Summary   71

6. IT'S OKAY TO ASK FOR HELP   73
   Fear of Looking Incompetent   75
   Asking for Help as a Strength Not a Weakness   76
   The Courage to Actually DO IT!   78
   8 Benefits to Facing Your Fear   82
   Chapter Summary   89

7. YOUR 30-DAY CONFIDENCE   91
   CHALLENGE
   Being Confident vs. Egotistical   96
   Increase Your Confidence In 30 Days   99
   Why You Deserve Happiness   110
   Chapter Summary   113

   Final Words   115

Introduction

"I have challenged fate to chess and am now attempting to keep all my confidence from puddling in my boots. What if I'm the only one betting on myself because everyone but me can see I am not suited to play at all?"

Mackenzi Lee

Do you have a nagging feeling that you are secretly bad at what you do? Maybe you don't trust your own abilities, and it has been stopping you from achieving your goals. Do you feel like a fraud? Or, maybe you can see that you have accomplished so much, but you are unable to internalize this success.

All of these feelings fall into the realm of **imposter syndrome (IS)**. Simply put, imposter syndrome is the belief that you are not as competent as others perceive you to be. It is much more complex than this, and we will discuss it fully in detail, defining the full characteristics and feelings associated with the syndrome. Fully understanding the beginnings of IS will help you to internalize why you experience the symptoms and just how many people do as well. If you are still uncertain about whether or not your individual symptoms align with this syndrome, we will also do some identifying to find key characteristics at play within your life.

You may be wondering, *Where does imposter syndrome come from?* The reasons behind it are different for everyone. It often overlaps with social anxiety. We will discuss the most common causes behind the beginnings of IS, and you will have the opportunity to find the most likely cause for you.

I am a hypnotherapist and executive coach and have worked in self-development all my life in the media industry. I work to help leaders and managers nurture self-confidence so they can become the best at what they do without doubting their own ability. We will do the same together throughout this book! We will first identify the problem and cause, then discuss techniques you can implement to overcome it. Rediscovering your self-confidence is a process, and we will have to be patient with ourselves! One of the toughest things about imposter feelings is the constant negativity. It can really take its toll on you. Let me be your guide to silencing your inner critic.

While there are many common symptoms of IS, every person experiences it differently. Their feelings may come and go, or they may be constant. A shocking 70 percent of people will experience the syndrome at some point in their life. There are also five specific types that are commonly associated with IS. You may fall into one of these: *The Perfectionist, The Superhero, The Expert, The Natural Genius, and The Soloist.*

Each of these types will be discussed in detail. You may find parallels in your own patterns of behavior, and discover specific ways to overcome your types of IS. All of us can have feelings of doubt and struggle with moving forward if we don't succeed right away. Setbacks or "failures" can cause imposter syndrome to creep into our life, but we don't want to let it take over.

There's nothing wrong with asking for help. When we are experiencing any kind of negative feelings, it's difficult to see things from another perspective. Let this guide be your outside perspective! We will focus on a *30-Day Confidence Challenge* that will help you build confidence and overcome insecurity. Everything takes time, but knowing that you have the tools and a plan to overcome your imposter feelings can help you get started on your path to stop feeling like a fraud and rebuild your strongest self.

ONE

What Imposter Syndrome Is

Truly understanding what imposter syndrome is and how it works in your life is a great way to begin combatting its effects. If we don't know how something affects us, how can we begin to change it? Imposter syndrome is the experience of feeling like a phony. You worry about being "found out" and that at any moment, believing that you don't belong where you are and have only been able to get there out of "luck. The interesting part about IS is that it can affect anyone no matter what line of work they are in, social status, or age.

The term imposter syndrome was first used by psychologists Suzanna Imes and Pauline Rose Clance in the 1970s. First thought to only apply to high-achieving women, the term has since become a widely recognized experience.

So, what are the exact symptoms? While IS is not a recognized disorder in the Diagnostic and Statistical Manual of Mental Disorders (DSM-5), it is experienced by at least 70 percent of people at one point in their life. They will have at least one episode of the phenomenon. It's important to note that IS was originally termed an imposter phenomenon. Clance told Amy Cuddy, Harvard social psychologist, that if she could do it all over again, she would have called it the "imposter experience" because it is not a mental illness or a syndrome, but it is something we all will experience. The definition of a syndrome is actually quite different from the true characteristics of imposter syndrome. **Syndrome** can be defined as a group of signs and symptoms that occur together and characterize a particular abnormality or condition.

While IS certainly contains a group of symptoms, they *may or may not* always occur together. They also do not characterize an abnormality. We all experience imposter syndrome! It does not mean we have an abnormality or a condition. Let's take a look at the specific symptoms/characteristics that align with imposter feelings so we can begin to identify where these come from.

Characteristics of IS

Some common signs to look out for include the following:

- self-doubt
- feeling like a fraud
- inability to realistically assess your own competence and skills
- attributing success to external factors or chalking it up to "luck"
- fear of being "found out"
- berating performance
- fear of living up to expectations
- overachieving to prove worthiness
- sabotaging success out of fear

- setting challenging goals then feeling disappointment when you fall short
- negative inner voice
- dwelling on past mistakes/failures
- constantly comparing yourself to others

Some of these symptoms may seem like a great way to motivate yourself to achieve, *but at what cost?* The pressure associated with IS is immense, and there is constant free floating anxiety that you will be unable to live up to the unrealistic expectations set for yourself. You may work extra hard (which is actually a specific type of IS we will talk about in Chapter 3). Working ourselves so hard may indicate that we need this external validation in order to feel worthy. Throughout this book, we will work on ways to cultivate our self-confidence so that this validation can come from within.

Much of this need for external validation may come from one of the symptoms: the fear of being "found out." You might be trying to prove that you are in fact not a fraud, when in reality, you are the only one thinking this way. This is exhausting, as you not only have to listen to those negative thoughts in your mind, but you are also trying to be a mind reader. As much as we all might like to, no one can read minds. It's tough to accept, but we cannot control what anyone else thinks about us. But, we *can* control what we think about ourselves. And this is what really matters. We need to be the one who is confident in order to internalize our success and not feel like a fake.

We want to enjoy our successes in life and be able to give ourselves credit. It's upsetting when we diminish our accomplishments by believing the only reason we got that promotion was because we appeased our boss or we only did well presenting our project because we skipped out on social events in order to ensure it was done perfectly. Even if you do everything "perfectly" you can still have imposter feelings. With IS, the more you do, the more you will experience IS.

Clance IP Test

Phew! What a terrible cycle! Don't worry. We will talk about all the ways to fight back against this. But, first, let's go over a few specific statements you may be able to relate to. During her studies of IS, Clance created the Clance Imposter Phenomenon Scale (CIPS) composed of 20 statements. Answers are based on 1-5:

- 1 (not true at all)
- 2 (rarely)
- 3 (sometimes)
- 4 (often)
- 5 (very true)

When reading the statements, you can score how true it is for yourself. Really focus on your answers to these. After answering all the following statements, add together your score for each one. If your total is less than 40, you have few IS characteristics. If between 41-60, you have moderate characteristics. Between 61-80 is frequent characteristics and higher than 80 is intense IS experience.

Clance IP Scale:

1. *I often succeed even after being afraid I would not do something well.*
2. *I can trick people into thinking I have more knowledge than I do.*
3. *I avoid having people critique and evaluate me at all costs.*
4. *When I do receive compliments, I worry that I won't live up to expectations.*
5. *Sometimes I think I gained all my achievements and success simply because I was "in the right place at the right time."*
6. *I'm afraid of being "found out" one day that I don't have the credentials I actually do.*
7. *I mostly remember the times when I have failed or not performed as well instead of the times when I have succeeded.*
8. *I rarely perform as well as I would like to.*
9. *Sometimes I feel that I've achieved things in life by mistake.*
10. *It's difficult for me to accept and internalize compliments from others.*
11. *Most of the time, I feel like I just got "lucky."*
12. *I'm disappointed with what I've done so far and feel I should have accomplished more by now.*
13. *I'm afraid to try new things because I'm afraid I'll fail, even though I usually excel when I tackle a new skill.*
14. *If I do well at something new and receive praise, I doubt that I will ever be able to accomplish it again.*
15. *I always diminish tasks I've worked hard to accomplish.*
16. *I feel that those around me are more competent and compare myself to their successes.*
17. *I worry about not succeeding and lack confidence in my abilities, even though people around me tell me I am competent.*
18. *If I have received a job offer or recognition, I wait to tell others until it is an absolute certainty.*

19. *If I am not the "best" or recognized as "special," I feel inferior.*

These statements are extremely specific. Answer them as honestly as possible. Knowing which ones resonate with you most will help you going forward in this book. You may find that you are often diminishing your accomplishments, or that you are lacking in confidence even though others around you believe in your abilities. If you had a high score on this scale, it may even be helpful to take a step further and talk to a therapist. Professionals bring a helpful outside perspective and can give you additional tools to combat the imposter feelings. Reading this book is a great start. You have decided to no longer live out these negative, doubtful thoughts, and take back control (Clance 1985).

What Causes IS?

Sadly, there is no one cause of imposter syndrome. It would be great if we could target that and put an end to it. But the feelings start for a variety of reasons. Also, people may feel them for the first time at different points in their lives. Some can remember them in childhood and have always experienced IS. Others may only notice it for the first time when there is a major change in life during adulthood.

Also, the original cause of your imposter syndrome may not be the cause of it now. Throughout life, we encounter different changes that can bring about imposter feelings. Maybe it's been years since you felt imposter feelings, or maybe you constantly feel them. No one is the same.

There are, however, several common causes that have been traced to IS. We will define several of them and look at some examples of them in action. See if you can connect with any of them and how they may be a cause of your imposter feelings.

Childhood Environment: So much of our behaviors and patterns can be traced back to childhood. Maybe your parents were overprotective or maybe they were underprotective. Children tend to develop imposter syndrome if there was a great deal of pressure to perform in school. They may have received harsh criticism if this expectation was not met or they may even have been compared to their siblings. Alternatively, your parents may not have played a huge role in your life as a child. You may have put pressure on yourself to perform in school or extracurricular activities in order to feel that external validation that was missing from your parents.

- *Example:* Brandon was a great soccer player in high school. His dad came to all his games and put a lot of pressure on him. He was recruited for the college team that he always dreamed of. When he got there, he saw that all of the other players were good too. Now when Brandon plays, he feels like he doesn't deserve to be there because he thinks everyone is so much better than him.

In this scenario, Brandon's father put pressure on him to perform, which he did. He eventually was recruited for the team he always wanted, but then felt like he didn't deserve to be there. He was a great player just like the rest, but somehow felt like he didn't belong. Without his father there to put the pressure on, he is now doing so for himself.

Personality Traits: Some people are simply more prone to imposter feelings. *Do you see yourself as a perfectionist?* IS and perfectionism go hand in hand. This is actually a type of IS, one we will talk about in the next chapter. But traits like this can be attributed to whether or not you experience IS. Maybe you have always been more prone to feeling anxious about your performance or to have low self-esteem in general. Some personality traits are part of our character and will always be who we are, but that does not mean we cannot work on them and be aware of them. Others, we can actually change for the better.

- *Example:* Sarah will be graduating top of her class. She holds herself to a high standard. Final grades are coming in and she has already received 100 percent on three out of four of them. When she receives her last grade, it is 95 percent. She will still finish at the top of her class by a landslide, but she gets upset, and starts crying at school. Her mother tells her that she should be proud of herself and she has done a great job. But, Sarah is unable to enjoy being top of her class and feels she does not deserve it after not getting all 100 percent.

Sarah is a great example of a perfectionist. Even though her mother tells her what a great job she's done, Sarah cannot internalize this. She pushes herself to be absolutely perfect and cannot even enjoy being top of the class because her grades were not 100 percent. Sarah can easily grow into adulthood and apply this same idea to her work, family life, relationships, etc. She is someone whose personality may make her imposter feelings more intense throughout her life.

Other Mental Health Problems: Underlying mental health problems can make imposter feelings more intense. If you are prone to certain mental health issues, you may also be prone to imposter syndrome. This can include mental health issues such as anxiety, depression, personality disorder, and more. Symptoms such as self-doubt and intensive worrying accompany many of these. Therefore, imposter feelings can sneak into the list of symptoms you experience overall. If you do have underlying mental health problems, it's important to seek out professional help. IS can sometimes be only a symptom of these other issues. It's important to address the primary problem first.

Social anxiety is a primary disorder that imposter syndrome overlaps with. Someone with social anxiety disorder (SAD) may feel like they don't belong in social or competitive situations. They may be in a constant state of worry, especially during social conversations. Not everyone with social anxiety will have imposter syndrome, but the symptoms of SAD can certainly help fuel imposter syndrome. It's good to be aware if you suffer from social anxiety or not because you can gauge your risk of imposter syndrome. You can also expect them to arise in certain situations, like the one below.

- *Example:* Tom just landed a job he has been trying to get for years. He starts in two weeks and his anxiety is overwhelming. He has been crippled with anxiety since he was a young child, and he now manages it with medication. But, with this new change, he is starting to become very anxious again and is having trouble sleeping. There are also some imposter feelings that are creeping in. He is wondering if there was a mistake. He even considers that they offered him the job by accident instead of a different applicant.

In this situation, Tom is used to his feelings of anxiety. When he has a big life change, though a positive one, he starts to not only feel anxious again, but to doubt himself. IS is known for making us believe that we do not deserve our accomplishments. Tom is not even able to enjoy that he got the job. There was no mistake, and he was the one offered the position. Yet, his imposter feelings try to convince him otherwise.

Life Changes: Speaking about new things, another big cause of IS can be major life changes. These changes can be good or bad, but anything that is different from what we are used to can alter our sense of self and our confidence. You may feel uncertain about moving to a new city or undeserving of a job you just rightfully earned.

- *Example:* Alicia is moving to a new city. She does freelance work mostly from home, so she can really work from anywhere. She has always wanted to move and be closer to the water. She was excited about it at first, but slowly she started to doubt her decision. She had thoughts that maybe she shouldn't leave and that she didn't deserve to move. This made no sense logically to Alicia, because she worked hard, and she always wanted to be by the water. But, she was unable to be excited for the move out of fear that she was unworthy of it. This was the first time she ever felt this way, and she started to wonder if she ever wanted to move in the first place.

In this situation, Alicia seems to be aware of her imposter feelings but still feels unworthy. She even goes so far to begin doubting if she ever wanted to move in the first place. Something good is happening to her, but she cannot internalize it. In a way, she is sabotaging the move out of fear.

Common Types of IS

There are a few different ways imposter syndrome can appear. While everyone experiences it differently, Dr. Valerie Young, an expert on imposter syndrome, categorized five subgroups. Many people are able to find similarities within at least one group. As we define each, try to think of situations in your own life that may line up with at least one type.

1. **The Perfectionist**: This type wants to be perfect. They get extremely upset when they do not reach the expectations they set for themselves. they may also be controlling and want to do everything themselves to make sure it is 100 percent.
2. **The Superwoman/man**: This type feels like they do not measure up. They push themselves extra hard and forsake hobbies and relationships in order to feel adequate. They may do work outside of their scheduled hours in order to feel competent.
3. **The Natural Genius**: Natural geniuses are used to completing things with ease. They learn new tasks quickly and do not have trouble when it comes to achieving success. Therefore when they find themselves struggling to learn something new, they feel less confident.
4. **The Expert**: The expert measures their worth based on what they know how to do. They seek out new

degrees and training in order to prove themselves worthy.

5. **The Soloist**: This type does everything alone. They hate asking for help and often feel incompetent when they have to do so.

Now that we have thoroughly defined imposter syndrome and how it can show up in your life, hopefully you are feeling better knowing what these feelings are. Sometimes identifying what these negative feelings are can alleviate some of the anxiety. Don't feel discouraged. Throughout this book, we will go over the different types in depth and tips and techniques to combat these symptoms effectively.

Chapter Summary

This chapter discusses the clear definition of imposter syndrome and the various characteristics that align with it. It's important to note that you do not need to experience every symptom in order to have imposter syndrome. The several causes of imposter syndrome are also discussed, and we talk about where the root cause of your imposter syndrome might be. There are five common types of imposter syndrome. Many people with IS fall into at least one type. In the following chapters, we will flesh out each type in detail.

TWO

How to Overcome Analysis - Paralysis

Perfectionism and imposter syndrome work together to create negative feelings. We want to overcome this and stop analyzing ourselves so harshly. We are all doing this in our own minds and will forever be our harshest critic. We can become so self-conscious of what other people are thinking about us, when in reality they are not thinking about us at all. If everyone is walking around worrying about themselves, then should we really be worried about what other people think of us? The answer is no. They are way more concerned about what they are doing. The perfectionist type of imposter syndrome is a very specific type that truly worries about reaching their own expectations. Then if they are unable to reach those expectations, they may worry about how that will be perceived by others. They are also focused on how well something is done. It can not be a 90 percent effort. There is no B grade for perfectionists.

If you feel you may be a perfectionist type, ask yourself these questions:

Do you have trouble delegating?

Have you been called a micromanager?

Do you feel like your work, relationships, and life in general has to be perfect all the time?

Does 99 percent equal failure?

Perfectionists set high goals for themselves, and when they can't reach them, feel like they are not good enough. Sarah, from the earlier example in Chapter One, is an example of the perfectionist type of imposter syndrome. This type likes to be in control. This is usually not out of malicious intent, but instead an attempt to make sure everything goes right. IS creates a feeling of uncertainty, and the perfectionist type works to fight that by making everything perfect.

Also, though perfectionists do tend to achieve lots of success, they can rarely enjoy it. Perfectionists will eventually experience burnout and be unhappy. They may work long hours, weekends, and still feel they are not doing enough. If a mistake is made and something does not go to plan, it is taken harshly. We have to learn to accept our mistakes. If we can accept them as a natural part of life, then it will be easier for us to accept failure or "less than perfect" results.

Steps to Overcome Perfectionism

I want to emphasize that there is nothing wrong with having expectations for yourself. Holding yourself to a certain moral standard can lead you to a positive lifestyle. It can also reflect your work ethic and help you be successful in your career. But perfectionism can be a toxic take on these positive expectations. Setting them too high can make them unrealistic, then when we don't reach them, we can feel bad. Perfectionism truly sets us up for failure, and instead of wanting everything to be perfect, we can work to notice the things we love about ourselves and accept the things we need to improve on.

Making mistakes should not be a terrifying idea. It is natural and how we learn. Think for a moment: Was there ever a time that you made a mistake and it actually was a good thing? Maybe you ended up learning something that helped you in the future, or you grew closer to a family member/friend through the experience? The ups and downs of life help make us who we are. Even when something feels terrible and there is no light at the end of the tunnel, we can find surprising positive outcomes. Without these low points in life, our character wouldn't be as strong. The phrase goes, "What doesn't kill you makes you stronger." And this is so true. While it doesn't necessarily have to be a life-and-death situation, the trials you face in your life will also make you stronger.

Even when perfectionists achieve something 100 percent, they are too stressed about continuing to do so that they cannot enjoy it. There is a moment of relief, and then right back to work! This is sad because perfectionists are usually very successful and work hard. They should be able to enjoy this and view all the hard work they do.

If too many mistakes or "imperfections" begin lining up, perfectionists may believe they are not as capable as other people. They may start to doubt their qualifications altogether. There are steps you can take to overcome and fight back against perfectionism. It's good to note that perfectionism is a personality trait, and it's not necessarily something that will be instantly cured. It is an ongoing process. You can work to retrain your mind to think about your accomplishments in a positive way and take back your confidence.

1. Recognize Behavior: Seeing perfectionism for what it is will help you begin to change your perspective. Many people view this trait as a good thing, which it can be. We have talked about how it can drive you to do more and be a competent worker. But in the long term, it will only cause damage to your self-esteem. Recognizing your specific thought patterns surrounding perfectionism is useful to finding your triggers. This trait may be a part of your character at this point and it will be difficult to reverse it. But these steps can help you get started and see that being imperfect is actually healthy.

Do you feel perfectionist tendencies at work?

Do your family dynamics make you push yourself to perform at 100 percent?

The source of perfectionist feelings can alter your life. Maybe when you were younger it was from your parents, but now you feel the pressure from work. The thoughts and feelings associated with perfectionism can make you feel depressed, anxious, or angry. These feelings can be heightened when you criticize yourself if you have spent so much time on a task but still believed it wasn't good enough. We want to change these automatic thought patterns toward ourselves.

Perfectionist thinking

- **Black/White Thinking or *Splitting:*** You may think everything is either all or nothing. Either the project you completed at work was a complete success or it was a failure. This is also called splitting, which is defined in psychology as when someone views their life in a false dichotomy. They see everything as either good or bad. We definitely want to avoid this, because it's simply not true. Not everything we strive for will be one or the other. Everyone "splits" in some aspect of their life, whether it be politics or sports teams, but doing so when it comes to self confidence and performance is damaging to the way you view yourself. There is certainly a gray area when it comes to being perfect, and that is because no human can be perfect. We can put on a facade of perfection, but only we know the truth.

- **Catastrophic Thinking**: This type of thinking is when you think of the worst-case scenario. Maybe you have a presentation coming up at work, and you think, "If I don't do well on this presentation, I won't be able to get over the embarrassment." or "If they see I am tired, I will look weak and lazy." This thinking does nothing for us. What's the good in imagining a negative outcome? If something is going to end badly, there is nothing we can do to prevent it. It is out of our hands. But, if we decide instead to look at it in a positive light, then we will be in a better mood, less stressed, and we may even perform better.

- **Probability Overestimation**: This thinking completely discounts any of the hard work that has been done. You may still think you won't do well even if you have prepared. Or, you chalk up all the hard work you did to luck. Maybe you assume something bad will happen even though you cannot possibly know the outcome. Or, even though you have put the effort in, you still think it will turn out bad. Maybe you really need help with some work around your house, but you don't want to reach out for help and be seen as less independent. You cannot possibly know what the other person is thinking, and we have to learn to give ourselves the chance to be imperfect and witness the true outcome before making any assumption.

- **Shoulds**: Ever feel like you should be doing something more? Perfectionists may have trouble allowing themselves time to relax. We all need time to destress, but that doesn't necessarily mean a perfectionist will allow themselves to do so. Using a should statement such as: "I should be cleaning now instead of watching a movie or I should work on that project again later. (Even if it's already complete, sometimes.)" Perfectionists may even feel that they should have known something would go wrong even if they couldn't have possibly prevented it. Many perfectionists will also compare themselves to what they *think* other people are doing. This is a primary symptom of IS. Imposter syndrome creates this comparison and concern for what others are doing. You may wonder if you are measuring up or if you even have the same knowledge as those around you.

- **Habit Formation**: These types of thinking are all habits. Habits are not just physical actions we do every day, but they are thoughts we allow as well. Think about all the habits you have in your life. Maybe you meet up with a certain friend on the same day every week. Do you have coffee right away in the morning or do you read the paper first? Maybe you eat a sandwich for lunch during the week but then something different on the weekend. We are creatures of habit and we form these within our thought process as well. We want to change the thoughts we have automatically. If you are a perfectionist, your first thought may always be *I could have done better* or *I'm not good enough*. Instead, try: *I did my best and gave it my all* and *I am worthy*. Working to change the narrative can break the perfectionist thinking and also work to fight back against the imposter feelings as well. While this will not change overnight, recognizing and being aware of these thought patterns can help us to change the negative ones to positive ones.

2. **Work on Realistic Thinking**: Now that we recognize our perfectionist tendencies and the negative thought patterns associated with it, we can begin to change our thinking. It's important to be realistic here and note that your perspective may not be the truth. This is a difficult thing to understand. As humans, we all have separate perspectives and see things differently. We could be participating in the same activity or even looking at the same color and experiencing it uniquely. This is actually such a gift! The best part is that we can alter

our perspective, and we can tap into our awareness to choose which perspective is the best to take in a given situation.

As we spoke about in the previous step, we will be replacing those automatic negative thoughts with positive ones. You may be so accustomed to these negative thoughts that you are uncertain what they look like. And, you may think they are true. They can be tricky, and almost veiled as encouragement to work harder. But, when they are constant and overly self-critical, it's time to replace them with more realistic ones. Let's take a look at some negative, critical thoughts you may experience, and then their opposite thoughts so you can try and identify some within your own mind.

I should be doing better! vs. *Nobody is perfect. I will do better next time.*

I can't believe I made that mistake. I'm so stupid. vs. *I messed up. But I learned something from it.*

If I don't get the promotion it means I am bad at my job. vs. *I will keep working hard to try for the next promotion if I don't get this one.*

Get that Perspective!: It's hard to look at things from another perspective. Our world is ours. And we are used to seeing things a certain way, thinking a certain way, and holding beliefs about who we are. But challenging this can only lead us to positive growth. Perfectionists often have a completely different view of themselves than others do. For example: Maybe you feel lazy because you only cleaned your house twice this week and you usually do it three times a week. You are noticing tiny things that others wouldn't. When you have some friends over, they mention how clean and neat your house is. We view others around us differently. It's good to keep this in mind. We are our harshest critics, and no one will be as hard on us as we are on ourselves.

Try questioning those perfectionist thoughts: *How would someone else view my home right now? What would they think about me staying up until 2 a.m. just to make sure that presentation is perfect? Would they think less of me if they knew I only exercised four times this week instead of five?*

Be Your Own Best Friend: What would you say to a friend who was going through the same thing? You would probably tell them to be kind to themselves and take a break. Try doing this for yourself from time to time. Be your friend, and treat yourself with kindness. Don't allow minor mistakes and setbacks to overshadow all your accomplishments. Would you congratulate your best friend on their achievement? Of course you would! Remember to do the same for yourself, and give credit when it's due.

Lean in to Catastrophe: Now this one might sound confusing. But go ahead, think about the worst case scenario. Think, what if? What if I don't work out five times a week anymore. What's the absolute worst that could happen? What if I don't do my absolute 100% best on that presentation or get that promotion? Does it really matter? This is a great way to get perspective because we can get so bogged down with the little things that we don't stop to simply think: What if? The perfectionist type is so afraid of imperfection, though they are unaware of what that really looks like. If you ask "What if?" you may find the answer is not all that scary. Sometimes what we are imagining is way worse than reality.

Compromising: Your black-and-white thinking may be overwhelming. You may need to compromise with yourself. Setting some more realistic expectations will help you be more flexible with your standards. If you have been finding that you lack the time to do those five workouts a week, then set the bar at four. Four workouts is still very impressive, and will certainly give your body the proper exercise it needs. It will feel strange when you first start lowering your expectations. You may feel like you are selling yourself short. But you can ask yourself what you can tolerate today. Every day our emotions change, and one day you may be feeling more up to challenging your perfectionism than another. Be aware of this, and on the days you feel really great, work to compromise.

3. Change those behaviors: Perfectionism can be compared to a phobia. Are you afraid of heights or spiders? Your fear toward these things can be similar to your fear surrounding imperfectionism. But, just like heights and spiders, we may come across imperfection at some point. The best way to deal with this is accept the inevitable and even strive to break our fear. Fear can be paralyzing and all consuming. This is one of the worst parts of perfectionism. It truly is all consuming. You may think about something that wasn't quite right from years ago, and find yourself ruminating on it at random times. In order to overcome this, we have to let some imperfection into our life. Try to see this as a good thing, because it will creep in one way or another. This way, you can have control over what areas in your life are imperfect. While there are plenty of ways you can try to be imperfect, here are a few examples that may help you see an area in your life where you can do the same.

Example #1: Time imperfection

- Kelly is always on time. It has been years since she has been late for anything. Her life is on a very tight schedule, and she has noticed that after church on Sunday, before her exercise class, she always rushes out to be right on time. She hates the feeling associated with being late to anything. But, she has been chatting with other people at church and always has to cut the conversation short. She decides to ease up and continue talking to some new people she met, which makes her a few minutes late to her exercise class. However, the people from church invite her to dinner that week and she begins fostering new friendships.

This is a great example of how we easing up on ourselves can bring great results along with a fresh perspective. Kelly may never have been invited to dinner if she rushed out before the invitation had a chance to be extended. She made a great choice in this scenario to stick around a bit longer and show up late to her exercise class. Though she will have to deal with the embarrassment of showing up a few minutes late, it will ultimately be worth it for the new friendships she is making.

Example #2: Honest imperfection

- John is a strong man. He is always there for his friends and family whenever they need him. They know he is reliable and caring. He rarely talks about his own problems or worries, even when his friends and family ask him how he is doing. When John is out to lunch with his friend, Owen, he is feeling stressed about his job. Owen can sense something is wrong, but thinks he should not ask because John does not usually share. John hates being seen as "weak" and considers doing what he normally would and not being honest about how he is feeling that day. But instead, he tells Owen his true feelings, and Owen listens. He then gives John advice that he finds very useful. John is surprised at how helpful Owen was and how much better speaking with him made him feel. In the future, he continues to confide in Owen and their friendship grows stronger.

By telling Owen his true feelings, John is more honest with both his friend and himself. John's primary concern was not appearing "weak." But Owen, being the good friend that he was, didn't want to pry because he knows John usually didn't like to share. After sharing, John realized that Owen wasn't going to view him as weak and that he was extremely helpful. In both this scenario and the previous one, small decisions for "imperfection" allowed for big positive outcomes. This is what we want to strive for. When we see small imperfections that don't make our world come crashing down, we may decide to rid ourselves of perfectionism altogether.

4. Prioritize Schedule: The perfectionist type may over-commit to several activities a week and find trouble fitting everything into their schedule. Try prioritizing what really matters. What do you actually want to do? This step is all about discovering what you really want, and not what you think other people want to see you do. This should also not be where you set unrealistic expectations for yourself, but a chance for you to set a schedule you can enjoy! Don't look at what other people are doing, but find what works best for you. Only you can truly know the best option for yourself.

5. Set Priorities: Understanding your specific priorities is a useful tool for life in general. This applies to all aspects. When we can see our priorities and always keep them at the forefront of our mind, they can have an effect on every decision we make. This is actually exactly what we want. We don't want to make decisions based on how we feel or what we think we want in the moment, but on the long-term effect it will have on our life. Priorities will look different for everyone. Try this:

Make a list of your top five priorities. They can be general such as family, work, health, exercise, school. Write them down somewhere you can access easily. A phone is a good place to do this because we all carry our phones everywhere we go. Then, the next time you are faced with a decision where you must choose between one task or another, look at the list and see which one more closely aligns with your priorities.

While this may seem like a simple or silly task, it is extremely useful. We can get so bogged down with daily life that we forget what is important. For people struggling with imposter feelings, your mind can be clogged with negative thinking and it's more difficult to make decisions. Simple exercises like this one can clear the mind fog and help you focus on what's really important. The perfectionist type may struggle with deciding where to devote their time and energy because they are so consumed with worry about every single thing being perfect. This is where the schedule setting comes in. Pick one or two things you can get done at a time. And, remind yourself that not everything you set out to do will be perfect. But if you keep your priorities in mind, you will naturally devote more energy to those things, and they will get better. You can learn to appreciate these more, and have less worry over non-priorities.

6. Reward Yourself!: Changing negative patterns and facing your fears is hard work. Be sure to take time and reward yourself. The perfectionist type usually dislikes downtime as they feel they should always be doing something. It can be exhausting in our own minds. It is okay to do a little "mind numbing" and watch some Netflix, play video games, grab dinner with friends, or whatever else helps you just relax. Giving yourself time to reset is crucial to performance. Therefore, perfectionists really should take this time if they want to be at their best.

Chapter Summary

The perfectionist type feels they must do everything at 100 percent in order to prove their worth and competency. Many perfectionists have difficulty delegating and tend to micromanage. We discussed several steps you can take today to overcome this feeling and begin thinking realistically. Several fictional examples were used that you can transfer into your own personal experience.

THREE

Imposter Workaholics

The second type of imposter syndrome, the super-man/woman type, is always doing more to prove they are worthy of their titles. They feel the need to excel in their life in all different roles. They may hold a demanding career, be a parent, a husband/wife. Within these roles, they may feel like phonies. Even if they are doing all they possibly can, performing well at their role professionally and being a great parent, they still feel like a phony. Feeling like a fraud is a common symptom of IS. It can be confusing, because even though you may be able to see all the accomplishments in your life, you simply cannot internalize them. The superhero imposter usually overworks themselves to cover up their insecurities. This is damaging to both their self-esteem and the way they relate to others. This creates a constant fear of being found out. This is unfair to yourself and creates anxiety over something that is not real. Have you ever felt like no matter what you do it's still not enough? This IS type is tricky because superheroes are supposed to be helpful and have a positive contribution. But, you may find that your superhero tendencies are causing extra stress in your life. If you feel you may be the superhero type, ask yourself the following questions:

Do you work later than many of your colleagues just to be certain the work you did during the day is good enough?

Do you struggle to have downtime because you feel like you should be working/doing something more?

Are you missing out on social events or forsaking your hobbies in order to work more?

Do you feel like you don't deserve certain aspects of your life even though you have the degrees and the hard work to prove you do?

Have you lost relationships or are there relationships in your life struggling from your constant need to be working?

There are many reasons superheroes feel the need to continuously be working. But, the main reason is due to imposter workaholism. They are addicted to the validation that comes from working. Have you ever completed a task that used a great deal of your time and effort? Think about how they made you feel. You probably felt accomplished and validated. Maybe it even made you feel more worthy of the job/position you hold. This feeling is exactly what this IS type seeks. Imposter feelings will create low self-esteem and the feelings associated with accomplishing work will help boost this. For superheroes, it's crucial to learn to find validation from within instead of from work. We cannot allow outside factors to have too much control over us. If we do, it can lead to negative factors in so many aspects of our lives, not just our self-esteem. Let's look at some negative effects of imposter workaholism and then ways we can overcome it so they do not completely rule our lives.

- **Low self-esteem**: This is an obvious problem associated with the superhero type. Ironically, the superhero does not feel like a superhero themselves. They may get validation from other people who see their hard work, but they won't ever feel this way themselves. With outside validation being the only thing adding to their self-esteem, alone time is not something superheroes look forward to. We need to be able to function on our own. There are times in life when we have to be the one to pick ourselves up and keep going. But, if we only gain self-confidence from external sources, this will not work. Our self-esteem has to come from within. And, it is ultimately this internal validation that keeps us going during the difficult times in our life.

- **Unhealthy boundaries**: There are two primary types of boundaries we are going to discuss: inner and outer. Outer boundaries are those we have with other people and inner boundaries are those we have with ourselves. In more detail:

▶ **Inner**: Inner boundaries include our emotions and internal world. These boundaries control the effect the external world has on our thoughts, feelings, and actions. Having strong inner boundaries is crucial to maintaining a strong sense of self. This way, the outside world cannot negatively impact the way we see ourselves or our self-esteem. As imposter workaholics, we may not be able to set limits within ourselves. Maybe we know that we need the day off, but we just won't take it off because we want to get ahead and make sure our work is good enough. And, accepting criticism, especially about our performance, is not something that is easy to do. We may take it to heart and feel that we are not competent. We will go over steps to help improve these inner boundaries.

▶ **Outer**: These boundaries are between you and other people. Outer boundaries help us set limits around how others engage with us. This includes physically, mentally, and emotionally. As superheroes, we may have trouble saying "no." We may always say yes to doing more at work or to doing more for our family members. Knowing ourselves well enough and saying "no" when necessary is important to fostering healthy outer boundaries.

- **Unhealthy Social Relationships**: Without healthy boundaries, we cannot possibly have healthy relationships. These relationships may be familial, romantic, professional, or friendships. When we cannot set boundaries, it allows for negative dynamics to creep in. Many superheroes will be "used" for their dedication at work. This can lead to exhaustion. In romantic relationships, superheroes may find themselves in unhealthy situations where they give so much emotionally, and their partner continues to take. It's important to be aware here of the relationships in your life. Do you feel you are always the one doing more? Do you go out of your way for those in your life but don't feel you get the same in return? Some superheroes do this of their own free will, because it is simply who they are. For others, they have fallen into this trap with their relationship and are now expected to behave a certain way by the other individual. Maybe you always worked harder at work due to your IS, and now your boss expects it.

Or, maybe you were the one to do all the housework in your relationship because you wanted it done right and like the validation, but now you are exhausted and your partner will not contribute. The scenarios are endless, but try to see where this may be applicable in your life. Throughout this chapter, we will discuss ways you can combat these feelings and begin to set healthy boundaries in your life.

- **Burnout**: No one can work all the time. You will burn out! This is a very common result of overworking yourself. Have you ever felt like you just cannot do a single thing more? Maybe you have finally completed that unrealistic 80-hour work week you set for yourself, and you want to go out with your friends. But, you are just too tired to do it. You are burned out. Or you may even see your work performance dwindling due to working too hard for too long. It's healthy to take a break. Humans are not built to work all the time. That is why we sleep for several hours at night. Aside from the time we are sleeping, we need regular downtime too. During this time, we are able to access the activities that most connect us to our sense of self, which can only improve our self-esteem.

We want to avoid all of these negative effects. You may be used to the positive encouragement you receive from others around you and from the validation you feel when you work continuously. But, this is simply not sustainable. There are ways that you can still work hard and feel validation without all these negative effects as well.

How to Find Validation From Within

A huge problem with seeking validation from others is that every person is unique. Therefore, what might satisfy one person will not satisfy another. You may be doing your best and pleasing one person, yet another person will not be happy with the result. This is simply human nature. We all have different likes and dislikes.

1. Awareness: Much like the perfectionist type, the first step to changing the behavior is recognizing it. It's good to recognize where this need comes from. *Do you believe that you are not good enough? When people tell you that you are good enough, does it make you feel better?* Knowing when you seek approval is just as important too. Superheroes do not work hard only in their careers, but they may also do the same in other areas. Maybe you excel in parenting and devote all your energy to your children, or you might be in a demanding graduate program. Whatever the situation, try and raise your awareness to this. There are several ways to do this:

- **Keep a journal**: Write down the specific moments and emotions you have. This will help you recognize what is triggering your need for validation. A journal is a physical way to look back on your progress. You can see exactly where things are working and where they aren't. You can then use this data collected from your own life and use it to make a productive plan going forward.
- **Meditation/Mindfulness**: Sometimes clearing our mind helps us to see things how they really are. There is so much noise and busyness in our daily life,

and as an imposter workaholic, you may find that you cannot see past all of it. Taking 10-30 minutes out of your day to be quiet can be illuminating. Mindfulness can look different for everyone. Maybe you want to listen to a guided meditation or a few simple breathing exercises will do the trick for you. There are plenty of mindfulness apps you can download right on your phone. This way, no matter where you are, you will be able to take a few minutes to clear your thoughts.

- **Ask someone you trust**: We all need people who we can trust. Asking them about our behavior and things they may notice allows us to see ourselves objectively. They may have noticed something that we can't see. If we are going to ask someone about our behavior, we need to be open to listening to their answer. We can't ask for advice and then shut down something we don't want to hear.

There are plenty of other ways to be aware, but these tips will get you started. When we have engaged in certain behaviors for a period of time, it's difficult to change! But we can go slowly each day.

2. Work on Self-Worth: We talked about how low self-esteem is a negative effect of being an imposter workaholic. Working on that self-worth will improve this situation! Self-worth and self-validation go hand-in-hand. *How can we expect to feel worthy on our own if we cannot validate our own actions?* Validating yourself may feel strange at first if you have never learned to do so. If you are wondering how to go about validating yourself, there are several ways to do so:

- **Recognize your strengths & talents**: Think for a moment about what your strengths may be. Every human is born with some talent, whether something small or large. Your talent may be empathy, for example. Maybe you are able to really see how others are feeling and react appropriately to it. When we are judging ourselves, we often only see the negative aspects of ourselves. But, recognizing and acknowledging our talents can be a way to validate who we are.

- **Encourage yourself!**: Sometimes in life, you will be the only one who will encourage you. While this is not always the case, it's so crucial to know how to encourage yourself. When you are feeling down, you want to be able to build yourself back up. Life doesn't always go to plan, but it certainly doesn't mean that we should give up.

- **Say nice things out loud to yourself:** This may sound silly, but saying kind things out loud instead of in your mind can be the difference between you believing it and not believing it. Hearing it out loud will make it real! Are you uncertain what you can say to yourself? You may not know how to speak to yourself in an encouraging, kind way. Here are some examples:

"I did my best."

"It's okay to not feel great all the time."

"I am worthy just the way I am."

"I'm proud of myself and all I have accomplished."

"I work hard and deserve a break."

"My feelings matter."

"I trust myself."

"I like (blank) about myself."

- **Accept your limits**: Just like we all have strengths, we all have limits. Our limits do not necessarily have to be weaknesses, but sometimes they are. Accepting both our own personal limits and weaknesses can help you validate yourself. The perfectionist type may struggle with this specific tip, as accepting our imperfection as humans is difficult to do. The limits can also be internal and external. You may accept less internally from yourself, but put up with more from others. Try to match the two of these. Do not make crazy expectations for yourself and then allow other people to let you down. Also, don't expect others to live up to the same expectations you set for yourself. Everyone is human and will make mistakes. It's tricky to find the middle ground here, but with hard work it can be found.

- **Prioritize your needs**: When working on self-validation, it's completely okay to put yourself and your needs first! We need to learn how to do this. As superheroes, we are always trying to save others and find validation from doing so. We are workaholics, constantly trying to do more. But you may be pushing aside your own personal needs in order to do so. Maybe you haven't been able to exercise as much as you'd like, or you forsake your hobbies in order to get ahead. Down time is a necessity. It's time to prioritize this.

3. Fact Check Your Beliefs: All of us have individual beliefs and a moral code. But this is separate from the beliefs and ideas we hold about ourselves and the way the world perceives us every day. We may worry that we are viewed as incompetent or less qualified than those around us. This is where imposter feelings creep in. As imposter workaholics, it's easy to believe the thoughts that tell us if we simply work harder, then we will feel better. But these thoughts are not productive and will only lead us back down the path of seeking outside validation. Our brains are hardwired to center in on a thought that is easier, but not necessarily logical. When we feel less qualified, the natural reaction is to take steps that will make us feel more qualified, right? If we take it a step further and really stop and think about the reality, we can decide to react differently. The thoughts we have are simply that -- just thoughts. People struggling with imposter feelings often allow their thoughts to control behaviors. Let's look at the definition of the word "thought." This may seem trivial, but it's good to get to the basics sometimes, and truly understand why we allow thoughts to have such control over us. According to the Oxford Dictionary:

Thought: an idea or opinion produced by thinking, or occurring suddenly in the mind

Our thoughts are contained solely in our mind. They do not have any power unless we give that power to them. They also can "occur suddenly" and may not have any bearing on our actual surroundings. Knowing yourself and how you truly feel will help you decipher whether a thought you have is yours or not. Just because you are having a particular thought/idea does not mean it's yours! Ask yourself: *Where did this come from? Is this what I truly think? Whose idea is this?* This is a simple way you can begin deciphering which ideas you react to and which you push to the side.

4. Practice Self-Love: I'm sure you have heard this a hundred times. It seems that everywhere we look now, people are talking about self-love and accepting yourself for who you are. This can be difficult to do when it seems that even everyone around you is finding it easy to just suddenly find inner peace and love who they are. It's not that easy. Self-love takes work and continued dedication. It is an ongoing process all your life. We all go through periods of time when we feel super confident, as if nothing can stop us. And, we go through time when we are uncertain, self-conscious, and just down about life in general. This is a normal part of life. People who struggle with imposter syndrome may notice that their symptoms come and go, or they have them continuously and learn to manage them. Self-love looks different for everyone. There's plenty of things you can do to take care of yourself. Here are a few tips:

- **Find/Engage in Your Passions**: Imposter workaholics usually forget about their passions in order to focus on work/family. When validating ourselves, we need to engage in our passions! These are so crucial to tapping into our sense of self. Workaholics lose this sense of self when they throw their whole being into working all hours of the day. Some imposter workaholics may have been doing this for so long that they no longer know what their passions are. But it's never too late to discover something about yourself. You can try engaging in new activities. Maybe go to an exercise class or get out in nature by hiking or walking! There's endless ways to find new activities you may be interested in, but doing so will help you validate yourself as an individual separate from your work. This will help quiet the imposter voice in your mind.

- **Let Go of the Past**: Forgiving yourself and others is a way we can all move forward. Outside of the realm of imposter syndrome, doing so is a healthy step. But, when it comes to IS, if you harbor memories from the past when you didn't measure up to your expectations or those of others, you may be holding onto that. It may actually be the root cause of your actions now. You can find self-love and forgiveness through letting go of these past memories and moving forward, knowing that you are doing the best you can.

- **Gratitude**: Cultivating gratitude is such a positive way to see yourself and your life in a positive light. No matter how bad things are, there is always something to be grateful for. Even if it's something as small as the shining sun. There is always something small there. A journal here would be useful. Or, you can just use your phone. Keep a daily log, and try to write down something different every day. It doesn't matter how big or small the thing is, but simply that you are taking the time to recognize it. This further helps you to love yourself and combat those imposter feelings. IS is so negative all the time. Cultivating a bit of gratitude helps you to bring something positive to contrast the negativity.

- **Cut Out Toxic Relationships**: As we talked about earlier in the chapter, a negative effect of imposter workaholism is unhealthy relationships due to unhealthy boundaries. To enhance your self-love, those toxic relationships have to go. How can you quiet that negative inner voice if you continue to allow others to speak to you negatively? A constant external voice can be just as detrimental as an internal one. Making the choice to love yourself doesn't end with you. It begins with your choice and extends to the world around you. Fostering a positive environment for yourself is just as important as changing the narrative you hold for yourself.
- **Be Patient & Persistent**: Self-love is difficult to find when you're not used to being kind to yourself. It will take time to get used to and then time to implement. This is all a process. Ridding yourself of negative feelings and of IS will take time. So be kind to yourself and don't give up when setbacks happen. Because they will! But, each time you push through, know that you are one step closer.

5. Understand Your Need For Approval: So why do you want people to approve of your actions? The first step, awareness, is a great way to start noticing our behaviors. Now we can begin to understand why we act in this manner. Sometimes, a greater understanding of a problem can be the solution. Much of your behavior may stem from habit! Next time, before you look to someone else for advice or validation, ask yourself first. *What do I think of this situation? Do I think my work is good? Do I like this?* Rewiring our initial reaction can help guide us in the right direction. Some people struggling with imposter workaholism seek approval because they feel deep down that they really don't know what they are doing and fear they may get caught. Others just want to be liked and accepted.

6. Stop the Comparison: Comparing your experience to anyone else's is unproductive. We all have struggles. These may not be visible to you, but everyone is dealing with something. Many people keep their struggles inside because they don't want to be judged. So, if you are comparing your inner life to the outer life someone else is projecting, then you are not seeing the whole picture. You are a unique individual and your purpose will not be the same as someone else's purpose. Humans have always compared themselves to others. We do this for a variety of reasons. Sometimes it is out of genuine curiosity. Or, we want to make sure we are "on track" and doing similar things as another person. In other cases, we want to make ourselves feel better when we see another person struggling. But, when we notice they are actually "doing better" or are more successful, we get down on ourselves. As discussed many times, life has its ups and downs. Someone may be doing well now while you are not doing so great. This is okay. Give yourself a break and don't compare your journey to anyone else.

7. Notice Your Inner Voice: You know that little voice in your mind that reacts to the world around you throughout the day? Sometimes it encourages you. Or, it might say negative comments. Maybe, it warns you about something that just seems off. This is known as a gut feeling. Our inner voice is constantly at work. We cannot shut it off. But we can decide how we react to it, and we can train it. We also want to separate our own inner voice and gut feeling from imposter feelings. This is how we can begin to not only love ourselves more, but know ourselves better! Sadly, imposter thoughts can creep in here. Being able to decipher between your true voice and those imposter voices can be the differences between having good or bad self-esteem.

- **The critical voice (or imposter thoughts)**: This critical voice is the enemy inside all of our minds. For those with IS, it is those feelings of self-doubt and feeling like a fraud. But for someone struggling with anxiety, it might be worrying or obsessive ruminating thoughts instead. We all have a critical voice. And, even better, we can decide how we react to it. This voice is usually embedded from early childhood, just as IS is. A common misconception is that if we stop listening to that inner voice, then we will lose touch of our conscience (or gut feeling). But, this is not true. We cannot trust this critical voice whereas we can trust our conscience. Becoming aware of the distinction between the two is how we can conquer it. Have you ever had a negative thought and then suddenly slipped into an unhappy mood? This was likely due to the critical voice. You can notice this, and then make the conscious decision whether or not to listen to it.

Seeking validation from within is a long process. As you can see from these steps, there are many methods you can implement in your own life to begin. Do not be discouraged. This can absolutely be done. We have become accustomed to listening to those imposter feelings. With each day, we can retrain our thinking. You are not alone in this struggle. Avoid burning yourself out and discover how to love and accept who you are.

Chapter Summary

The superhero competency type falls into workaholism due to their need to always be working. They seek validation from outside sources, causing them to be burned out and left with no time for a social life. This can lead to unhealthy relationships and low self-esteem. For the superheroes, it's crucial that they find validation from within and discover their self-worth does not come from overworking themselves.

FOUR

When Trying Hard Becomes Too Much

The next type of imposter syndrome, The Expert, is always afraid of being exposed for being unknowledgeable. They base their own competence on how much they know they can do. This is tiring because we can't all know everything! It simply is impossible. But, when the expert finds that there is something they do not know, they feel like they are not worthy. There is always more for us to learn and striving to improve your skill set can help you professionally and improve your chances in the job market. But we don't want to take this too far. Seeking out too much information is actually a form of procrastination. Instead of sticking to one thing, the expert is always receiving additional degrees or certifications to prove that they are knowledgeable.

If you feel you may be the expert type, as yourself the following questions:

Are you always going for new degrees and certifications to gain knowledge?

Even if you hold a good professional position, do you still feel like you don't know enough or as much as your colleagues do?

Are you worried that people around you will find out one day that you don't know as much as you seem to?

Does it make you feel uncomfortable when someone calls you a professional or even an "expert?"

Do you refuse to apply to certain positions unless you hold every qualification?

If you answered yes to any or all of these questions, then you may fall into the expert type of imposter syndrome. This chapter will cover all the ways you can fight back against the imposter feelings associated with this specific type. Experts need to center their focus on accepting their skills. We only need to acquire a new skill when necessary. There's no need to get four Master's degrees in order to prove we are smart. If you don't know how to do something, you can ask a coworker. There's no shame in this. It may be hard to hear this for an expert, but we will discuss the ways you can start accepting it's okay to ask for help.

Often, experts have imposter feelings because they felt they were not good enough at some point. This can go all the way back to childhood. Many experts grew up feeling like they were not good enough. The environment in which you lived in as a child may have affected the way you view yourself and your competency.

Growing Up Feeling Not Good Enough

Our guardians hold great power over our psyche as children. The way we were raised absolutely influences us in our adulthood. But as adults, we now have the responsibility to be aware of this and change our actions/beliefs if necessary. There are many different scenarios in childhood that could have led to your feelings of incompetence.

1. Treated As Worthless or Sub-Human: This is a sad situation in which parents treat their child as less than human. They are abused physically, mentally, or sexually, and denied their basic human rights. This can permanently damage the psyche of a child and is detrimental to their growth. If you grew up in this environment, hopefully you are now in a safer and happier place. Therapy is an extremely useful tool and can help with the imposter feelings as well. You may have been expected to meet all the needs and wants of your parent/guardian and were berated when you were unable to do so. This can create the need to perform and to always know the right thing to do. You may feel the need to behave this way in your current life and automatically perform as an "expert" in all areas of your life.

2. Falsely Blamed & Held to Unrealistic Standards: If your parents/guardians were not mentally healthy, you may have been blamed for all the problems in the household. This is damaging because a child is never to blame for these things. This may have created confusion for you, and you may have felt like you should know more and be able to solve the problems. You may have also been held to extremely high standards. Maybe you were expected to get all As. If you received a 'B,' that was no good. We all have our strengths and weaknesses. And we all get less than an 'A' every now and then. Having guardians who don't understand this can make us feel inferior when we grow into adulthood. Imposter feelings create a need for high expectations. Experts want to prove they can be good enough and they may still be doing so to make up what happened in their childhood.

3. Compared To Others: We know from the previous chapter just what comparison can do! Everyone, and especially every child, grows and learns at a different pace. Children are compared to each other in so many ways. Parents may even say things like, "Why can't you be more like (blank)?" Verbally abusive parents may even say, "I wish I had (blank) as a son instead of you." This can make a child feel terrible and want to be better, to the point of obsession. They will go on to compare themselves as an adult and make sure they are measuring up to what other people are doing. This comparison makes children insecure and feel like they are not good enough just how they are. This same child then grows into adulthood feeling the need to compare themselves to others and prove their worthiness through additional knowledge.

4. Taught to Feel Helpless: Some guardians actually want their children to feel helpless so that they stay dependent on them for longer than usual. Children will then be dependent on their guardian for too long. This can be a form of **codependency**. Codependency is when two people are so invested in each other that they no longer know how to function without the other. They lose their sense of self and are only able to function with the other person. Their mood, happiness, and choices are all influenced and affected by the other person in the codependent relationship. This often happens with children and their parents. They may not even be allowed to make their own decisions or to explore and make mistakes. This sets them up for failure as they grow up because they will not know how to handle criticism or accept mistakes. Children may feel a lack of control in their own life. As adults, this same lack of control may still be felt. The adult may still be reliant on the parent in some ways because they were raised this way.

Listening to & Understanding Your Fear of Not Being Good Enough

Fear is not an inherently bad thing. While it is only a perception, it can be the perception that protects us from something harmful. We want to listen to our fear always and take the logical step to decide if it is something we want to react to. Certainly, if we are in a life-or-death situation, and that adrenaline flight-or-fight fear kicks in, we won't have much time to think it over. But when the fear is more psychological, based on feeling and memory, we can take the time to listen to it and understand what it is trying to communicate to us.

Fear uses what it knows to tell us something: feelings. When we sense fear, we are feeling its attempts to get our attention. So, you fear not being good enough? This doesn't have to mean you are actually not good enough. It simply means that something is being communicated to you. We are constantly receiving different communications. Some are internal. Maybe our neck is bothering us, so we are feeling pain. Maybe we are tired, so we are yawning and feeling sluggish. We are also receiving external communications from others every day. We pick up on body language, tone of voice, and just plain old verbal communication. The feeling and communication we receive from fear is no different. You may feel this fear for a variety of reasons:

- Your self-doubt stems from childhood trauma/experiences and still has an effect on you.
- People around you are putting down your goals and dreams, and you have started to internalize their words.
- You don't want to leave your comfort zone.
- You are afraid to accept your accomplishments because you may have failures in the future.

All of these are completely logical reasons to feel not good enough. But, we want to be realistic with ourselves. And, we want to give credit when it's due. If you are feeling like you're not good enough, then you're probably working pretty hard to prove that you are. But, you may still be busy putting yourself down. The tricky part about this is that our minds know everything about us. They know our secrets and our weak spots and those imposter thoughts will target them. We don't have to stay rooted in this fear of not being good enough. We can take steps to feel better about who we are and where we are in our lives every day.

How to Feel Good Enough About Yourself

We don't just want to feel "good enough" about ourselves, but we want to like who we are! This is easier said than done. We can't simply wake up one day and decide to like something, especially all the parts of ourselves we have spent time criticizing. We can take it slowly, and learn to see ourselves in a different light.

1. Remember Accomplishments: People struggling with IS will usually only recognize past failures. They skip over all the great things they have done and only focus on mistakes. It's easy to focus on the negative because they probably had the most impact on you. Try writing down some positives and when you do, close your eyes and remember how it made you feel. When you finally got that degree, or that position, or finished first in the race, how did it make you feel? That was all you! Your hard work and effort got you there and it will do so again regardless of any mistakes along the way. Focusing on these positive feelings can set you on the right path. If we constantly wallow in negative feelings and past failures, then it will be easier to say "I knew I couldn't do it!" if we fail again.

2. Volunteer/Uplift Others: We can get stuck in our mind. If you find yourself spending all day obsessing over whether you are good enough and forgetting about all you have to be grateful for, then you may need to step outside of yourself and help others. There are people struggling in the world in worse ways. Of course, this does not discount your feelings. Your struggles are just as relevant and valid as anyone else's. But seeing things from another person's perspective can help you keep your problems in check. In every city, there are plenty of opportunities to volunteer. You can look up some things online or go through your church if you belong to one. Uplifting others can have an effect on the way you view yourself too. You will feel more confident and good about yourself for helping others. It's truly a win-win situation.

3. Get Moving!: While not everyone likes to exercise, you can do small things to get out in nature and get the blood running through your veins. Our bodies are meant to move around and be active. Doing so activates our lungs and lets the oxygen get to our brains easier. This can clear our mind and open us up for more positive thinking. Endorphins, the "feel good" chemical, are also released during exercise. Even during a brief walk you can get some endorphins and help improve your mentality. Moving our body improves our overall physical health. There have been studies stating how the physical and mental mind connect. We can improve our emotions by improving our physicality.

4. Don't Set Expectations: Those struggling with IS have a problem with expectations. They set them way too high! It's a good thing to have big goals, but if you are unable to meet them right away, you shouldn't feel down on yourself. During this process to feel good enough again, try not to set any unnecessary expectations for yourself. Give yourself a break. Try for a week, month, or a few months to stop setting any expectations for yourself. Of course, you most likely still need to keep up with the basics in your life such as laundry, going to work, exercise, etc. But, don't try anything new or too difficult. You may be wondering why you shouldn't try something new.

And, this isn't forever. Giving your mind and body a break can actually help you to notice what you have in your life now.

5. Express Your Thoughts: Getting those negative thoughts out of your head is a great way to take away their power. Sometimes we just need someone to listen. If you have a trusted friend or family member who can help you sort out fact from fiction, then they will be a great resource to help you feel good about where you are. You can tell them exactly how you're feeling, and you may be shocked by how quickly they can help you see it in a new life. If you would rather keep these thoughts to yourself, then consider writing them down or saying them out loud. Taking them out of the realm of your mind can stop the rumination and take away the power they have over you. Sometimes, we just need to release the negativity.

Surrender to Not Knowing Everything

Sometimes all we can do is surrender. This does not mean that we completely give up, but instead that we decide to relinquish control. Letting go of control is such a freeing feeling. Doing so is difficult for all people struggling with IS, but it is something necessary for mental and emotional peace. The expert type must understand that even when they finally feel good enough and like their knowledge is valid, they still will never know everything. This may make the experts shudder but it needs to be recognized.

Surrendering can be a beautiful thing. It is letting go of resistance and allows for positivity to enter and lets you "go with the flow." We never know what could happen when we allow the path to open up instead of being so focused on the destination we think we are pursuing. It's okay to take those blinders off every now and then. Look around! Don't get so stuck on the goal you think you are trying to pursue. Here are some tips to surrender control:

- **Control vs. Contentment**: Trying to control everything is exhausting. And, it's simply not plausible. Control is thinking about everything in advance and your reaction to it instead of just letting life be. We might have a totally different experience if we give up control. Our contentment comes in when we can accept where we are. Just because we are at a certain point does not mean we will be there forever. But, if we are unable to accept it now, then we cannot move forward.

- **Patience in the Process**: Learning to trust the process allows us to give up the need to control every little step along the way. We are all a work in progress! Giving up control allows us to tap into what we have right this minute and simply appreciate it for what it is. This helps us place trust in our life and also helps us learn how to do so within ourselves. Many people struggling with IS simply do not trust their own judgement. Experts especially feel they lack the proper knowledge to function properly and therefore will do all they can to prove they are knowledgeable enough. The act of trusting also teaches us patience. Everything in today's world is so immediate. We can order food and receive it within a few minutes, send a quick text message to a friend, Google an answer we need and get it within 30 seconds. It's hard to wait for something. Trusting in the process teaches us to wait for the good to come.

- **Quiet the Restlessness**: A feeling of restlessness goes hand-in-hand with a lack of patience. Maybe we want to see a change happen but we don't see the results yet. Or, we have an expectation of something and it doesn't seem to be working out that way. Creating inner peace will quiet this restlessness. In order to create this inner peace, we must let go of the past and future and only exist in the present. To exist in the present, we can:

  ○ Deep breathing

  ○ Music

  ○ Reading

  ○ Mindfulness practices

  ○ Nature

Surrendering is one of the most difficult practices for people with imposter syndrome. It's difficult for all people in general. But once we start feeling good about ourselves and where we are in this moment, it will get easier. Experts should not feel discouraged about their tendencies. It's admirable to recognize you can always learn more. But, it's equally as important to cultivate gratitude for what you know and where your life is right now.

Chapter Summary

The expert competency type bases their worth on how much they know. They are constantly receiving new degrees and certifications out of fear of being exposed as unknowledgeable. This constant need to keep learning can quickly turn into a form of procrastination. For this type, it's critical that they surrender to not knowing everything and be present in their current situation.

FIVE

When You Don't Succeed On Your First Try

The Natural Genius competence type struggles when they don't succeed the first time they try something. They judge their competence based on how easily and quickly they can adapt to new skills. In contrast to the superhero, they are not so concerned with how much effort it takes, but how easily they can do it. They are also not concerned with any degrees or certifications needed. They actually love being able to know something without those things. If the natural genius takes too long to learn something, she will feel ashamed. Similar to the perfectionist, natural geniuses have incredibly high expectations for themselves. None of us can possibly succeed with *everything* on our first try. If we could, life would be so much easier. In order for natural geniuses to overcome these tendencies, they have to see themselves as a work in progress. This philosophy applies for all of the competency types. IS makes us believe that we should be at the top of our game all the time. But this creates shame and guilt over ideals that are impossible for anyone to meet. Instead of expecting to get things right the first time, we will learn to identify certain behaviors we can improve over a period of time. If you think you may be the natural genius type, ask yourself the following questions:

Did you get straight As in school and now excel in all your professional positions?

Do you achieve your goals without much effort?

Are you opposed to having help because you would rather do things on your own and prove that you can?

If you face criticism or are unable to complete something the first time, do you feel ashamed and not good enough?

Do you avoid doing tasks you haven't tried before?

Does the thought of learning something you've never tried before intimidate you?

If these questions resonate with you, then you may hold yourself to high standards that are causing you to feel guilty. We want to work through this and find a healthier way to relate to our successes and failures. They are both a natural part of the process. Putting in effort and learning new skills are crucial to personal development. If you are not prioritizing this, then you may be sabotaging your own development.

How Natural Geniuses Hold Themselves Back

1. Expecting Raw Talent: Some people are born with natural talents. Maybe they excel in sports or academics without much effort. Natural geniuses often do so in their childhood, but then find it harder to do so as they grow older. The competition gets more intense and they find other people around them working extra hard to succeed. Having an expectation for raw talent to carry you throughout life may leave you feeling disappointed. Working at our skills is a necessary part of life. We have to cherish our talents but also use them in order to keep them active.

- *Example:* Kyle was extremely smart in high school. He excelled in math and science. Now, he is in his twenties and struggling to find a job. He checks LinkedIn to see that other people from his class are excelling in their career. Many of them went on to get several more degrees and are now engineers. He feels ashamed and wonders why he is not as good as they are anymore.

▶ In this situation, we see Mark, a natural genius, suddenly feeling like he is doing something wrong and not as good as those from school. There are a few things happening here. Mark is comparing himself to others and viewing social media. As we talked about in the previous chapter, comparisons are never a good idea. And, social media never shows the full story! So, these two actions are opening the door for imposter feelings to set in. Mark is also holding himself to the standards of others and expecting to be where they are. His path is different from his classmates and he may not be meant to do the same thing as them.

▶ **Try this**: If you see your peers excelling in areas you once found easy to perform in, really be honest with yourself and understand why this is. Have you worked on your skill over the years? Could you maybe use a little brush-up? Many people don't want to go back to school after a certain age. But, it's never too late to go back. Try to identify specific areas where you can improve. For Mark, going back to school may be one of them.

2. Neglecting Other Skills for the Sake of Intellect: Natural geniuses often push aside other social skills, like healthy relationships and friendship, in order to focus on the success of their intellect. When you were younger, maybe your parents even prioritized intellect over social relationships. Did you spend weekends with friends or did you spend them studying? This can be detrimental because often children will grow up to hold the same mentality. Of course workplaces need professionalism, but they also need people who are personable!

- *Example:* Rachel is a lawyer. She wins almost all of her cases with ease and expects her employees to always perform at their best. She has not seen her friends in a while because she is always working and taking on new cases. She loves the feeling of winning a case and the validation she receives from it. Her colleagues are always praising her, telling her that she is a genius and they don't know how she does it. But eventually, her friends stop inviting her out. She checks Facebook to see them posting pictures online while out to dinner.

▶ Social relationships often struggle when imposter syndrome is involved. Rachel may not have noticed she was brushing off her social relationships until her friends stopped inviting her out. Having relationships outside of work is crucial to personal development. We want to avoid Rachel's behavior and be sure we aren't investing all of our time into our intellect.

▶ **Try this**: Limit the amount of validation you seek from your accomplishments. While this seems like a simple task, you may become accustomed to the feeling of "performing well" and not just performing well, but doing so with ease. Try remembering the activities in your life that you *like* doing. The important distinction here is that these activities may not necessarily be things you are good about, but are simply things you enjoy!

3. Get Bored Easily: Maybe you find mundane tasks boring. If you are not being stimulated intellectually, or with a skill you enjoy and excel in, then you may get bored. This can apply to all different skills. A natural genius who excels in math may get bored at a baseball game. Alternatively, a natural genius who excels in baseball may actually hate math class. This is damaging because you will hold yourself back from experiencing new things. Boredom may become a habit as well. If you don't "think" you are being stimulated with something, then you may not even try. *How can you ever try something new if this is your attitude?*

- *Example:* Matt is a great football player. He excelled in high school. He was the starting quarterback as a freshman and then became team captain by his junior year. He was then recruited to a Division 1 school, but he sat the bench the first season. He found that everyone around him was good too. He tried to focus on school, but he found that he actually did not know how to do a lot of the work in his classes because he did not pay much attention in high school. School bored him and he would skate by, doing just enough so he could continue playing football. Now in his college courses, his grades started dropping, and he started to wonder what was wrong with him.

▶ In this example, Matt is used to excelling. He was bored by school and did not put much effort into it because he was a natural genius in football. Then, when he achieved his goal and made it to college, it was not what he thought it would be. And, because he did not focus on any skill besides the one that came easy to him, he was not able to do well in his classes.

▶ **Try this**: Look at the big picture instead of focusing on one particular skill. As humans, we can have many interests and things we are "good" at but not necessarily "genius level." You don't have to expect top performance from yourself in all areas. This will actually lead to the boredom you feel in other areas. Try devoting some time each week to other activities you would normally find boring. This could be something as simple as reading, riding a bike, or just listening to music. This will train your mind to focus on something other than your natural talent.

4. Overthinking: Natural geniuses do a lot of thinking. They consider themselves geniuses after all. So they are constantly using their brain. However, we want to be sure that it's not too much. Now this may sound strange to you -- how can I think too much? There comes a point when we spend too much time thinking about something that it becomes an obsession and we spend the whole day ruminating on our thoughts. This is definitely something we want to avoid, because this can actually be a form of procrastination. Instead of making the best decision possible in the moment, often natural geniuses may overthink their decision to ensure they get it right the first time.

- **Example:** Joanne just got promoted. She knows she should be happy about it, but she is feeling stressed. She is not catching onto this role as quickly as her previous. When she first joined the marketing firm, she quickly climbed the ladder. Now, she has to manage several other employees and is finding it overwhelming. There is a due date coming up for a client and she is unsure how to handle the project. She spends several days obsessing over it instead of asking her manager for help. She misses the deadline and the client is upset.

▶ Here we see Joanne struggling in her new position. She decides that she would rather struggle in silence and overthink a possible solution instead of asking for help. This is something the natural genius and the soloist competence type struggle with specifically.

▶ **Try this**: Take note of your thoughts, and when regular in-depth thinking turns to rumination. Ruminating can take over our life and distract us from being productive. A good tool if you find yourself overthinking is to make snap decisions. You can practice this at the grocery store or while cleaning the house. We don't always have to make decisions in a moment's notice, but this will help train your brain to make them quicker and with less obsession.

5. **Refusing Teamwork:** Speaking of asking for help, refusing teamwork is another way natural geniuses make things harder for themselves. They would rather work alone

and judge how easily they can complete a task by themselves rather than be seen as needing any kind of help. While it feels good to do something alone, there is nothing wrong with asking for help. This may come off wrong to your coworkers as well. You may be viewed as selfish or cocky. While your other coworkers work together and complete things quicker, you may hold yourself and your coworkers back by taking longer to complete a project that could have been done together.

- **Example**: Michael is the point guard on his college basketball team. There are 15 seconds left on the clock and they are down by two. The coach tells Michael they should run the play for another teammate to score two points and win the game. But, Michael is usually the one who makes the most points and who helps win the game. He wonders if the coach doesn't think he is a good player anymore. So, when the game starts, he immediately shoots a three-point shot to try and win. He wants to prove he is still a good player. He ends up missing, and his team loses the game. His teammates are furious with him.

▶ Michael took the final play personally. He thought his coach didn't think he was worthy of making the final shot. So, he set out to prove his worth and ended up losing the game for his teammates.

▶ **Try this**: Notice why you don't want help from others. For those struggling with imposter feelings, it is usually because they don't want to be viewed as incompetent. But, take the time to decipher between your inner critic and your own thoughts. Then, reach out! You may find positive effects in doing so. You will cultivate more trust, stronger relationships, and a whole world outside of your own mind.

Misconceptions Surrounding Natural Geniuses

When we hear about really successful people, it's difficult not to compare ourselves to them. We also never get the full story. We only hear about what great achievements they have and how much money they make now. But, we don't see all the hard work behind this achievement. They may have worked 80 hour weeks to get where they are now. We also don't see the failures. We have to fail in order to succeed! How else would we learn the right way to do something?

Even natural geniuses have to work hard! You may have a natural talent or gift, but it's still something you have to work on and foster over time. Everything in this world is constantly evolving. We as people must do the same thing. It's okay to not know everything and feel confused now and then. This actually opens up a space for new skills and learning to come in. Take Bill Gates for example. He dropped out of Harvard and was the co-owner of a failed business before starting Microsoft. He is now a millionaire. This is why it's so important to fact-check our beliefs. We may see other people in a certain light without knowing the full truth behind it. There are some simple things you can start doing today to give yourself a break and accept that you may not know how to do everything right the first time around.

Admit You Don't Know It All & Embrace Learning

1. Listen: Many natural geniuses simply do not listen. This could be at work, in social situations, or at home with their partner. Becoming a better listener is something we can all do. Do you ever feel like you are just waiting for your turn to talk and not really listening? Being an active listener can help you learn something. If we are just waiting for our turn to talk, then we are not truly taking in what the other person is saying. This is not only rude to the other person, but it also limits our communication skills. Active listening necessities include:

- Body language
- Providing feedback
- Being nonjudgmental
- Undivided attention

2. Ask Questions: You can ask questions while you are practicing your active listening. This is two steps in one. Doing so is a great way to learn something new. Many natural geniuses feel shame in asking questions. They don't want to appear knowledgeable. Have you ever been at work and wanted to ask something, but didn't want to be judged? Many bosses would actually prefer that you ask a question to clarify something. This way, it ensures that you care about the work and that the work will be completed correctly. It also shows that you are actively listening to what is going on. You may find that you have more and more questions as you become involved. This is a good thing. Your work can benefit greatly from involving other people.

3. Be Humble: Maybe you are already successful in a certain field or position. But, you are reading this because you still have imposter feelings surrounding your natural talent. This is actually a great time to be humble. Acknowledge your skills, but also acknowledge the hard work and skills of those around you. This will heighten your self-awareness and your awareness of the success of others around you. Nothing bad can come of being humble. We don't want to diminish our accomplishments here, but instead notice that there is always room for improvement and time to learn.

4. Respect: Along with humility comes respect. We want to be respectful of other people and their experience. Maybe they were not born with the same skill set or talent as you. Instead of correcting or tuning out others with different opinions, try opening yourself up to new ideas! When we respect others, they in turn respect us. Nothing bad can come from having this approach to others.

5. Body Language Awareness: *Has anyone ever told you that you look upset or angry when you are just sitting?* Being aware of how body language comes off to other people is a great way to be more respectful and open to learning. People will make judgements before they even hear another person speak based on whether they appear open to dialogue! If you look closed off, sitting with your arms crossed and brows furrowed, then people may not want to approach you.

These are just a few tips to help you realize it's okay to not know it all. Being a natural genius has its advantages and disadvantages. It can be great to excel in a particular area, but this is not the end goal! We can continue to improve upon that skill throughout our life, and yes, even learn new ones! Hopefully you are feeling a bit better after reading through this chapter. The imposter feelings surrounding the natural genius type do not have to control your life and stop you from moving forward.

Chapter Summary

The natural genius competence type bases their proficiency on how easily and quickly they can learn/complete something. If they do not get it right on the first try, then they feel unworthy. Many natural geniuses were able to learn new skills quickly in their childhood or young adult years, but may now struggle to do so. This type must learn to admit we cannot know how to do everything. Unlike the expert, they need to be open to learning more and expanding their current knowledge.

SIX

It's Okay to Ask for Help

The last competence type of IS is The Soloist. This type is afraid to ask for help out of fear that it will only expose them as a fraud. While there is nothing wrong with being independent, we don't want to do so to the extent that not asking for help is used to prove our worth. The soloist is different from the natural genius in this way. They do not have to get things right the first time, but if they don't, they certainly won't ask for assistance the second time around! There should be no shame or guilt associated in asking for help when needed. Still, both are felt by the soloist. Though similar, the two are distinct. Shame is a feeling that your whole being is wrong, and it is not associated with any specific event. But guilt is that feeling you get when you think you've done something wrong. It doesn't necessarily mean you have done something wrong. Many people with IS struggle with shame. They always feel their being is incorrect and that they are phony. But, not all imposters feel guilt. The soloists definitely feel guilt after asking for help. This is why they avoid it at all costs. If you think you may be the soloist type, ask yourself the following questions:

Do you feel the need to accomplish everything on your own?

Do you feel guilty after you ask for help, even if you really need it?

Does not asking for assistance make you feel worthy?

Are you validated by completing difficult tasks alone that most people could not do by themselves?

If you do ask for assistance, do you ask more so for the task/event itself rather than for your personal needs?

All of these feelings are associated with the soloist. If this is how your imposter feelings manifest, don't be discouraged! We can always grow and learn to accept help. The natural genius needs to learn in other ways. They will learn to cultivate their natural skill over time, and you will be able to learn to ask for help. Doing so seems like an easy fix, but once your validation and self-worth becomes rooted in not doing so, it can be a big change to suddenly begin reaching out. It can be another version of fear. In Chapter Four, we talked about the expert and their fear of not being good enough. But this fear applies for all competence types. For soloists specifically, they hold a fear of looking stupid. They worry about how they will be perceived by those around them. This is why their self-esteem and worth is firmly rooted in not reaching out. Reaching out would be a form of surrendering, of acknowledging that they do not know as much as they appear to. But, does this fear of looking unknowledgeable actually make you look more unknowledgeable?

Fear of Looking Incompetent

In a report from 2014 released by Harvard Business school and the Wharton School, findings showed that many people are actually afraid to ask for advice and risk looking incompetent. But, according to the study, their thinking is incorrect. They actually will be viewed as more competent by the people they are asking if they take the time to ask for help.

There were a series of studies within this report that were used to come to this conclusion. Participants were told to imagine they needed advice from a coworker and imagine how competent they thought their coworker would view them as if they were to ask for help. It wasn't surprising that many of the participants imagined they would be seen as less competent if they asked for help.

This makes total sense. Especially for the soloist. We don't want it to appear that we don't know anything, especially in front of others. But in the next study, participants were paired with a partner and could only communicate through instant message. The interesting aspect to this study was that there was no other partner and the participants were only communicating with messages pre-programmed by the researchers. Participants then took a test. Some were asked for their advice by their "partner" on that same test and others were not. The participants then rated their "partners" competency. The participants who were asked for advice actually rated their "partners" higher in competence.

Going a step further, the study requested the participants rate their self-confidence after the test and those who were asked for advice had a higher self-esteem. This study seems to show that asking for help is a win-win for both parties involved! So, just because you may think doing so makes you less competent, it actually does the opposite. Not only this, but it improves the way you are viewed by the other person and boosts everyone's self-esteem.

There is a human quality to asking for help. We all have insecurities and struggles we keep inside. When we extend this "insecurity" or awareness that we need assistance, we are being more honest with ourselves and those around us. This can only make us appear more genuine and knowledgeable about life itself.

Asking for Help as a Strength Not a Weakness

So, what truly constitutes a character strength vs. weakness? According to *Character Strengths and Values: A Handbook and Classification*, there are 24 character strengths which are all under six broad virtues. This book was written by Dr. Martin Seligman and Dr. Neil Mayerson. They created the Values in Action (VIA) Institute on Character. It wasn't until later that social scientists identified the six virtues. The best part about these virtues is that people are able to score higher in one of the six areas, but it does not necessarily mean that they are not strong in the other areas. The VIA focuses on what is working in people's lives and the other strength areas that they can work on. Let's take a look at the six virtues and the character strengths that fall under each one.

1. Wisdom: Cognitive strengths which allow you to learn new things and use prior knowledge in creative ways.

- Creativity
- Curiosity

- Open-Mindedness
- Love of Learning
- Perspective

2. Courage: Emotional strength in the face of turbulence and opposition. Both external and internal.

- Honesty
- Bravery
- Persistence
- Zest

3. Humanity: Ability to care for and connect deeply with other people.

- Kindness
- Love
- Social Intelligence

4. Justice: Passion for civil rights.

- Fairness
- Leadership
- Teamwork

5. Temperance: Positive judgements.

- Forgiveness
- Modesty
- Prudence
- Self-Regulation

6. Transcendence: Connections with the universe, nature, religion. Stronger sense of purpose and understanding.

- Appreciation of Beauty
- Gratitude
- Hope
- Humor
- Religiousness

According to these virtues and the strengths associated with each one, asking for help would absolutely be a strength instead of a weakness. It would most likely fall under the Humanity and Temperance virtues. When we ask for assistance, we are forming deeper relationships with those around us, tapping into our humanity. And, we are acting modestly, regulating our inner life and recognizing we do not know all the answers. Not only this, but reaching out to others is a huge act of courage. We don't always know how asking will be received. But in doing so, we are being our true, honest selves. And just by doing so, we are already on a positive path.

The Courage to Actually DO IT!

Now that we see the strength in asking for help, it's time to find the courage to do it. But what if you're not sure where to even start? That is okay. We have a plan. There are a few steps you can take when there's something you need help with, and you know you want to ask, but your IS is holding you back. Those imposter feelings are so sinister, because even when we give in and do all the actions to get validation, they still come back! And, we are left feeling not good enough. Taking back the control of your life is the only way to shut the imposter feelings down for good. Let's look at some steps you can start taking today:

1. Be In the Right Mindset: Sometimes we simply are not ready to make a change. You may be thinking, Wait, I thought we were changing right now? And yes, we can. But only you truly know yourself. It's great you have made the courageous choice to read this book and start looking for more positive ways to cope, but only you know if it's the right time. If you have too many other stressors in your life right now, then it might not be the best time for a huge change! When we are deciding to do something different, it's always a good idea to start slow. Especially if you are still uncertain about this, take some time to think about it and decide why you want to stop feeling these imposter feelings. Are you tired of doing everything by yourself? Do you have burnout? You may have so many negative thoughts still circling in your mind that it's difficult to even get in the right mindset to make a change. Try this: Find your why. Why exactly is it you're doing this? Maybe you want to have more energy to be around your family more. Maybe you want to reconnect with your friends. Maybe your relationship has suffered because you don't share things with them anymore, feeling like you have to take it on yourself. Whatever your reason is, try to tap into it. Once you have a specific reason, or reasons, that you have decided to work on this, then you know you are in the right mindset to start.

2. Prepare Your Speech!: While you may not be giving an actual speech, it's good to prepare what you will be saying to someone when asking for help. If you will be talking to your spouse about needing help with bills or housework, prepare what you're going to say. This is a great time to use "I statements" in which you begin with, "I would really like some help with the chores each week because I'm feeling overwhelmed." Instead of saying, "You never help around this place, and you need to do more." This will make whoever we are communicating with feel attacked and our plea for help may not be accepted the way we are hoping.

3. Watch Others: If you work in an office setting, you can observe how others ask for help. Do they email your boss with some questions? Do they make an appointment with their manager to discuss their questions and concerns? Are they curious and engaging when they ask? For some soloists, the problem becomes that they *no longer know how to ask for help*. After a long period of time, they may realize they are ready, but they have suddenly forgotten how to ask! Observing the way others find the courage and carry out their questions can be a great opportunity for you to emulate their behavior. It will also allow you to see that they do not spontaneously combust after asking!

4. Take an Alternative Perspective: Many times, soloists will take asking for help personally even if it is for a greater cause. Try to look at it from the outside. How will this improve the situation of others, or of your work, if you do ask for help? Maybe your client will be more satisfied with the project if you ensure it is completely correct. Or, maybe your company will have better reviews. If you have become so accustomed to not reaching out, then it may be hard to even imagine another perspective. This is where Step #3 comes in handy. Really observe not only how other people ask for help, but what happens when they do. Whatever the effect, try to see your part in it as just that: a part to a greater whole.

5. Do Your Research: Before you ask for help, make sure you have done everything you can to ensure you tried your best. At work, if you do not try your hardest first, your superior may view your questions as lazy. But, if you are a soloist, then it's doubtful that you did not do your research. Most soloists will do everything they can to complete a task by themselves before even thinking of asking for help. So, this tip is just a gentle reminder for you soloists.

6. Consider the Effect of Not Asking: So you've decided you're not going to ask. Maybe it's help with taking the kids to all their practices, or with a work project, or even with something emotionally you've been dealing with all by yourself. Consider what will happen if you don't ask. Will it make you feel better or worse? The outcome will most likely be negative not only for you, but for others. If you don't share what is bothering you, then your interpersonal relationships may struggle. If you don't ask for help on your new assignment, you may be penalized for not completing it correctly. There are many times in life when we have to weigh the positives and negatives. Though it might make us uncomfortable or doubtful, we have to push that aside and do what will have the best outcome.

7. Face Your Fear: This fear is one that has been controlling you for a long time. It's time to face it. The benefits of doing so are endless. In the next section, we will talk about why it's so important to do so, and how you can focus your mindset on the benefits instead of your fear in the moment.

8 Benefits to Facing Your Fear

1. Sharing Your Gifts: When we finally ask for help, we can share our gifts with others and they can share their gifts with us. You might even discover something new. Sharing experiences is a part of being human. Sadly, if we are closed off to asking for help, then we are closed off to experiencing the gifts other people have to offer. We also cannot fully share ours because we are not being our most genuine and true self.

- *Example:* Janet has been knitting for years. She owns her own online store and has many clients. She is having trouble with a new pattern that was requested, but she knows that her sister has experience in this type of pattern. She doesn't want to seem unprofessional for asking her sister, as her sister does not own a store. But she decides to put her insecurity aside and ask for her help. Her sister is happy to help and shows her a few other pattern techniques while explaining the one Janet originally asked for.

  ▶ Our gifts can be big or small. We never know how sharing that gift will turn out. Janet made a great choice and decided to be honest about her lack of knowledge. Her sister then was able to share her knowledge about several different types of patterns.

2. Opportunity for Others: When you open up to receiving help, you are giving someone else the opportunity to make a difference. Maybe they have been looking for the opportunity to make a change, but they just haven't had the opportunity! This is why it's so important for soloists to realize that when they make the choice to go at life alone, they are not only harming themselves! Through facing your fear and asking for help, you are allowing someone else to use their skills and make a difference in your life.

- *Example:* Brandon has been struggling for a while. He has been noticing that his anxiety is high regarding his studies. He is a biology major and his program is very demanding. His college is a few hours from his home, so he only talks to his mom on the phone about once a week. He doesn't want to let her know how he really feels, so he usually tells her everything is going great when they talk on the phone. But in reality, things are not going well. She can sense something is wrong. He finally tells her on the phone one day, and she helps him find a therapist specializing in anxiety near his school.

  ▶ Sharing his true feelings had a great benefit in Brandon's life. He was able to confide in his mother, who could sense something was wrong. She was looking to help him but couldn't until he reached out for help. This is a huge benefit of reaching out!

3. Awareness of Strengths: Reaching out for extra help actually helps us to see the areas we are stronger in. It raises our self-awareness. Knowing the areas we need help in can highlight the areas we don't need help in. It will allow us to acknowledge the parts of ourselves that are strong! So often, people with IS do not recognize their strengths and instead only see the negative parts.

- *Example:* Alex recently started a new position as a copywriter. He is finding writing copy for social media easy, and he is always ahead of schedule. But, he's finding the assignments for SEO keywords difficult. He is worried about what his superiors will think as he just started the position. He excelled in many of his previous positions and has never felt at such a loss. He thinks about it for a few days, and then decides to contact his superior. She assures him that he is doing a great job, especially with the social media assignments, and she sets up several meetings to go over SEO with him.

▶ Alex did the right thing here! When we ask for help, many times we also can see our positives. Just because we need to improve in one area, does not mean all our other areas are not good enough. It actually means the complete opposite. Alex's superior even mentioned how great he was doing with the social media assignments and was happy to help him learn.

4. Realistic Expectations: Many soloists don't reach out to others because they overestimate how much effort it will take to do so or what kind of reaction the other person will have. We can blow things completely out of proportion in our own mind. A huge benefit of reaching out for help is that we may realize it will take a lot less effort to ask, and our request may be received better than imagined.

- *Example:* Julie's kids are messy. The house is full of clothes and dirt. Her parents are coming to visit and she only has Friday evening to clean up the place. She works a demanding job and stays later because she likes to finish her work for the week by herself, ensuring it is all done correctly. She gets home to see how bad the house looks. She thinks about not even asking her teenagers to clean up, but then decides there is no way she can do it alone. She goes to each of them and asks them to do a different section of the house. Surprisingly, they agree and are willing to help her.

▶ We never know how people will react! Especially when it comes to kids, they may not be the most helpful all the time. But, if we don't ask, then we will never know. Julie was able to have realistic expectations toward how much work had to be done around her house, and in turn asked her kids to help.

5. Better Communication: When we have to ask for help, proper communication is crucial. Through reaching out, we are automatically working on our communication skills. We communicate in so many different ways: verbal, nonverbal, visual, written. But, the main type will be verbal communication when asking for help. This will improve each time we make the choice to be open with someone else.

- *Example:* Tom and Anne have been together for five years. Tom doesn't usually say when he is feeling down, but lately he's noticed that his negative feelings have been overwhelming. Anne knows something is wrong, but she doesn't want to ask him because she knows he likes to deal with things alone. Tom is also aware that Anne is there for him. He decides to talk to her because he cannot handle his feelings alone anymore. When he tells her, she embraces him and they spend several days making a plan of what to do going forward.

▶ Here we see the communication between Tom and Anne strengthening. It's clear that they already have pretty strong nonverbal communication. Anne can sense something is wrong, and Tom knows that he will be there for her when he needs something. But, he takes it one step further this time and verbally expresses to her the feelings he is having. We can always strengthen communication with those in our life that we love and care for. Sharing our true needs and wants with them will only help this process.

6. Stop Feeling Like You "Owe" People Something: Many soloists feel that they owe themselves something. Or, that they owe the imposter feelings something. They may not consciously be aware that they are trying to alleviate their imposter feelings by going at life alone, but this is what is happening. When you put this feeling aside and allow yourself to share with others, you can stop feeling like you owe something. If this isn't enough for you, and it's still difficult to let people help you, try beating the system by helping someone else first! If you offer your skills and strengths before asking for help, it may alleviate some of the stress you feel around owing them something.

- *Example:* Andrew is moving out of his apartment to a new house. He is really proud of himself for being able to afford the house, and he has done everything on his own to get to this point. But, he knows he will need help moving. He doesn't like this idea because he just wants to get in the new house and show people how successful he is on his own. A few weeks before his big move, he helps his younger brother who is moving out of his parents' house and into his first apartment. Then, he asks if his brother will help him.

▶ Sometimes, we have to play a little game with those imposter feelings. Instead of completely giving in and trying to move to a big house all by himself, Andrew alleviated his feelings of "owing" his brother something by helping him first. This, too, was a win-win situation for them because he volunteered his time to help someone else and was then able to ask for help.

7. The Sooner You Reach Out, The Less Help You May Need: We don't want to overthink asking for help! In certain situations, if you ask for help early enough, you may actually be able to cut down on the amount of help you need. This would be ideal especially if you are feeling uncertain about asking in the first place.

- *Example:* James has been working on his thesis for his doctorate. He is uncertain if it's headed in the right direction. It's at the beginning stages and he knows he should go to his advisor to make sure it's right. His thesis needs to be correct in order for him to pass the program. James has never had to ask for help as he has done very well in all his courses without any help. But, he decides it would be worth it to go ask just this one time. When he does, he finds out he was actually on the wrong track, and he would have failed if he didn't reach out to his advisor.

▶ This scenario is a great example of how when we ask soon, it can save us later. If James didn't ask, then his whole thesis would have been a failure. This is a great benefit of reaching out. We just never know how helpful the other person will be for us. Their perspective could change the way we see a problem and help us overcome the situation way earlier.

8. Higher Self-Esteem & Positivity: Overall, you will just feel better. There is so much anxiety surrounding doing things alone. Soloists are much like perfectionists in this way. It's hard to live like this! It's definitely not fun. Making the choice to open up, be vulnerable, and express your need for help is a difficult one, but it will permanently change your life and the way you relate to yourself and other people.

- *Example:* Amy has been struggling with money lately. She is in between jobs and knows she will not make her rent this month. She has been living out of her parent's house for two years since graduating college. Her mom is always asking her how she is doing, if she needs anything, etc. She found the apartment herself and had a great job when she first moved out. But, the company downsized and they cut her position. She doesn't want to tell her mom because she is afraid she won't be proud anymore. But, the due date for her rent is coming up, and she finally tells her mom, crying to her on the phone. Her mother tells her how proud she is and tells her about her experiences when she first moved out. It makes Amy feel so much better knowing she isn't the only one to go through this. Her mother helps her with rent and is there for her emotionally.

▶ In this situation, Amy was able to realize she was far from alone. We all go through tough times in life, and these are the times to lean on people we trust. She had the faith in her mom to eventually tell her, and it worked out in her favor. Amy felt better about her situation and her mother was happy that her daughter shared the truth with her.

As a soloist, hopefully you are now feeling better about your situation. You don't have to forever live a lonely life where you need to do it all! Facing our fears is a natural part of self-growth. We need each other as humans, and connecting emotionally is healthy. The benefits of being courageous and asking for help are endless. But, this list touches on some of the most important ones. In the final chapter, we will discuss a solid plan all competence types can use to gain back your confidence and overcome insecurity.

Chapter Summary

The soloist strives to complete everything by themselves. If they are unable to complete something alone, then they feel they are not competent. But, the soloist must learn that it's okay to ask for help. We all need it. We talked about the six character virtues, and how asking for help is classified as a strength, not a weakness. And we discussed how to find the courage to actually take the step to reach out to others.

SEVEN

Your 30-Day Confidence Challenge

There are times in life when we all lack confidence. Life will knock us down, but it is within all of us to overcome this. IS can make this extra hard. It can make us doubt ourselves even when we do accomplish our goals. This is because IS increases our insecurities that are already there. Because the syndrome can read our mind, it knows our deepest insecurities. It knows just how to push our buttons and make us feel bad. So why do we have such a hard time dealing with these insecurities? Can't we simply recognize them as insecurities and decide to ignore them? If only it were this simple. There are many reasons that get in the way of us overcoming insecurities and moving forward.

1. Need for approval: The Expert and Superhero may relate most to this. When you feel a need to be accepted, it's hard to ignore those parts about you that get in the way of doing well. It's great when other people validate who we are, but if that's the only way we feel good, it can quickly become a problem when it comes to our personal self-esteem. We will read into every little detail and fear rejection in all that we do. With a higher need for approval comes more elevated insecurities. When the stakes are higher to perform well, we will become an even harsher critic of ourselves (yes, it's possible). This will actually hold us back from performing our best because we will be so focused on insecurities other people are not even aware of.

2. No Trust: If you have been wronged in the past, it can be hard to make others see your point of view. This can lead you to feel insecure about your thoughts and feelings. You may wonder if you have the wrong perception about other things too. This is why trust is so important. Having those around you that will help you fight your insecurities instead of feeding them can make all the difference. But just because one person or a few people have let you down does not make everything you think invalid. You also have to make the decision for yourself about what is real and not. Your feelings and thoughts are real. Do not let another person validate them for you.

3. Critiques from the Past: Maybe we have received harsh criticism before and are now finding insecurities within ourselves that we never noticed before. Or, due to these criticisms, we find it difficult to focus on anything but our insecurities. It can be a downward spiral when people point out something that we already do not like about ourselves. In some cases, the environment we grew up in can also be a factor. If we were bullied or had relatives that always criticized what we did, then of course we will struggle with our own self-image. This way of thinking is ingrained in us. This inner critic may actually be the same voice of that relative or friend who hurt us in the past.

4. Unhealthy Self-Image: And, speaking of self-image, it's likely we have taken criticisms received and internalized them, feeding them to our inner critic and allowing them to take over. This cultivates an unhealthy, and false, self-image. The true version of ourselves is imperfect, but not made up of our criticisms. We do not want to reject any part of who we are. Maybe we don't like a characteristic about our personality or something about our body, but these are all parts to our whole self. Rejecting these things only makes us more insecure.

5. Social Media: Everything we see only can make us feel insecure. Whether it is someone doing well in their career or someone with a great body, we are constantly comparing ourselves. We want to stop this compare-and-despair cycle. Because most of the time, those pictures being posted do not reflect reality. Models, influencers, celebrities are well known for using Photoshop and applications that greatly alter their appearance, then when real photos are taken of them in public, they look completely different. Something to keep in mind here is that famous people are people too. They have insecurities and may feel the same pressure to live up to standards as we do.

So how can we deal with this? If there are all these reasons and more for why we feel insecure, what is there to do about it? It can be difficult to stop feeling insecure. It becomes an automatic reaction and prevents us from trying new things, pushing through adversity and holding healthy self-esteem. But, what holds us back from overcoming our insecurities may also create an opportunity to develop critical skills to deal with them. If we embrace all the reasons above and become mindful of them, we can use it as a way to work on our negative emotions. How we can do this:

- **Work On Finding Approval From Yourself:** When you feel that little twinge of needing approval, take a moment to notice your body and thoughts. Notice what's happening that you don't like. *Why are you feeling so insecure right now? What is it about yourself that you are needing approval for?* Allow yourself to fully see these parts of you. This may be difficult, but you may actually find that these parts are not all that bad! Maybe you even like them, and your insecurities about them are not truly coming from you, but from one of the reasons listed above. Reassure yourself and embrace these things. Doing this does not mean you will never need approval or love from others, because we all need this sometimes. But, it means that you will be *okay* without it. You learn to be good with you!

- **Cultivate Trust in Each Moment:** We can't always trust that everything will work okay. But if we live in the moment, day by day, then we can take things one step at a time. Trust takes a great deal of time to build, but we can decide: "This will be okay." If this thought comes true, then we can slowly build up trust. This goes for all aspects of life such as relationships with others, with ourselves, work, etc. If we are always feeling insecure, then we are already assuming failure. Trusting that small things will work out allows us to work our way up to the big things.

- **Let Go of Past Experiences:** Negative criticisms and memories where our insecurities got the best of us may still play on a loop. Letting go of these experiences will allow you to move forward. We all are imperfect, and if you find yourself continuing to harbor resentment toward someone who said a negative comment to you a long time ago, try to imagine what they may be feeling. This is difficult to do, especially when they have hurt us. But, we all feel insecure. Even the most successful, beautiful, and smart people on this planet. This is exactly what imposter syndrome does. Those who have done well may feel worse. Therefore, those who upset you in the past may not have been in the right, but it will only benefit you to let go of that experience and forgive. Holding onto the situation is poisoning your inner life and keeping you trapped in that same insecure feeling.

- **Stop the Comparison:** Learn to focus on yourself. Take a break from social media if you need to. Remember that we all have a different path in life. Just because you are not "as successful" as someone else right now does not mean your path will not take you to another success in the future. None of us can truly predict what the future holds. Look at both yourself and those you compare yourself to as one in the same. You are both people with insecurities and individual struggles. A little compassion for yourself and others here can go a long way.

Being Confident vs. Egotistical

Many of us struggling with imposter syndrome worry that we will come off as egotistical. We struggle to accept compliments. Sometimes this is because we truly feel that we do not deserve these compliments and other times it is because we are worried about how others are perceiving us. But, this holds us back from being confident! Our confidence is crucial to self-growth and happiness in life.

A strong sense of confidence is what allows a person to become whole. Without it, you may find yourself pulled back and forth in different directions. You may morph into different versions of yourself just to appease whoever you are around at that time. But, you don't stick up for yourself out of fear of appearing egotistical and selfish.

It's important to make the distinction between ego and confidence. Ego is only about the self. Having a big ego means you only worry about your own self-interest and often put yourself before others. It can be very selfish. In contrast, confidence is about having faith in yourself and your abilities. This is something IS causes us to struggle with. As we work through the steps to build up our confidence, we want to make sure our ego does not get in the way. It's natural to get defensive when we face criticism. But, this may come off the wrong way to others around us. Here are some tips:

- **Drop Your Defensiveness**: It's difficult to face criticism. Have you ever felt your body tense up when someone says something negative about your character, actions, or you in general? When this happens, we want to take a moment and process this information. We definitely do not want to immediately respond with the first thing that pops into our mind. This might not be the most productive answer. It can cause more conflict and we may say something we don't actually mean. Instead, take some time to process the information and decide if it is useful to you! You know yourself best. Just because someone else has a criticism for you does not mean it is accurate. This is part of confidence. Each person has their own perspective and opinions. In life, it's true that you will like some people and not like others. Similarly, other people will like you and not like you. This is not something that is your fault and it's not something you have to fix. It's just life. While you can't control this, you can control your reaction to them. You do not need to yell back or react impulsively.

- **Hold Back Judgement**: We all have perceptions of other people. But, we never truly know what is going on inside of anyone else. Everyone deals with struggles and problems we can't see. So, if we hold back our judgement, we have a new appreciation for how other people are behaving. What insecurities does the other person have? How are they feeling today? Changing our automatic judgement to a positive one allows us to be kinder to other people, but it can also help us be kinder to ourselves when we make mistakes. Instead of immediately putting ourselves down, we may take the same approach we do to strangers around us. We can ask ourselves, What insecurities am I having right now? How am I feeling? It takes a long time to break this bad habit and replace it with a good one. As humans, we all make judgments when we first meet someone or when we hear news about another person. But cultivating compassion around the behaviors of other people will lead us toward more positivity.

- **Focus On the Process**: Instead of looking for the end result, focus on the work. Do you want to be more confident in all areas of your life or one specifically? Why do you want to be more confident? Understanding your driving force behind these feelings will allow you to appreciate the process more. Along the way, you can learn more about what works and doesn't work for you. In each process, there are steps. You will stumble and fall. It won't be a smooth ride, but it will be something you can work on. And hard work feels good. If you don't like hard work now, at the end of this process hopefully you will learn to have an appreciation toward the work it took you to get here.

Now that we fully understand that we are striving for confidence, why we feel insecure, and the ways we can overcome it, it's time to get into our 30-Day Confidence Challenge! Just like we have talked about, this is all a process. It takes time to retrain the way you look at your behavior and accomplishments. Putting too much pressure on yourself will not help you succeed. There are little things you can do each day to step outside your comfort zone and find the strength within yourself to become confident.

Increase Your Confidence In 30 Days

Day #1: Take Control of Online Influences

The accounts and images we look at online have a huge influence on our insecurities. If there are certain people, profiles, accounts or anything online that makes you feel bad, unfollow them now. Becoming aware of the influences around us can help us become more aware of our internal life. The internet is damaging because it can be accessed at any time. Even in the safety of your own home, it can make you feel bad. This is the time to take control of that feeling.

Day #2: Wear What You Like!

The "fashionable" clothing is always changing. You may find yourself trying to fit in and wear what your peers are wearing. But do you really like these clothes? If you don't, then you simply will not feel confident or comfortable in them. Start wearing what you like. Don't worry about what is "fashionable" or "cool" but wear what you enjoy. This will give you the confidence to be yourself. The more you can be yourself and feel comfortable in your own skin, the easier it will be for you to stand up for yourself and what you need.

Day #3: Decipher Between Useful Thoughts

When those imposter thoughts begin sneaking in, make sure to sort them out. Is this your inner critic? Is this how you really think about yourself? Also, note if it is useful to you or not. Will this thought help you stay on the positive track? If not, then don't pay any mind to that negative thought. Not every thought we have is useful. Have you ever had a random thought and wondered, where did that come from? Our brain is constantly working to process the information and world around us. It is then our job to use our conscious mind to sift through what is truly useful for us.

Day #4: Recognize If the Rejection You Feel Is Accurate

As people who struggle with IS, we often feel rejected if we do not live up to the expectations in our head. But, we can also feel this rejection coming from outside sources. Try to step back from these situations and understand if you really are being rejected or not. Is this other person really pushing you away or are you feeling hurt by your perception of the situation? Try to stay grounded in reality in these moments. Others may not realize you are feeling rejected. This may be a great time to work on communication with those you care about. Be direct! Ask them, "Were you ignoring me in (blank) situation" or "I felt shut down after (blank)."

Day #5: Take Up Space!

Be who you are and don't shrink yourself down to appease others. Many people with IS stay quiet or will physically try to take up less space out of fear of how they will be perceived. This is damaging to your sense of self because you may start to act how you believe others want you to. You are a unique person. Be confident. Take up space! State what you feel and don't hold back today. Even if you only do this for one day, it will boost your confidence that much more.

Day #6: Let Go of One Thing

If something has been weighing you down for a long time, let go of it today. This could be something big or small. We all carry around things and have trouble letting go of grudges or stressors. Pick one of them today. Decide how you are going to let go of this thing. Are you going to delete an old number of someone who hurt you? Are you going to stop ruminating over a situation from weeks ago? This will clear up space in your mind to allow positivity to enter. We want all the available space to do the hard work and live a healthy, imposter-free lifestyle. Focusing on grudges will do nothing but hold us back.

Day #7: Do Something Exciting

Get your blood pumping! Life is meant to be lived and enjoyed. Your IS may hold you back from doing many of these exciting things. If only for today, do something exciting. Have you always wanted to hike that trail near your home? Or, maybe you've always had a dream to skydive. During this healing process is the time to finally try these exciting adventures. It's all about you and discovering the things that make you feel alive and most like yourself.

Day #8: Accept Where You Are Now

Everyone has goals and an idea of where they want to be. This is healthy and necessary for continued growth! But, we cannot move forward if we don't accept where we are now. Make peace with the process and enjoy being in the present. You don't want to look so far ahead that you are unable to be present in your current situation. Think about what you enjoy about your life now. Are you really enjoying your job? Your friends? Even the weather? It may sound silly, but there is always something in your current situation you can find that is enjoyable. Once you do this, you will be able to move on to the next step of your life.

Day #9: Stay Off Social Media

For one whole day, stay completely off social media. Put your phone away for the day if you have to. When you do this, take note of how you feel. Write it down to remind yourself. Are you less stressed? Are you more engaged in the people and events happening around you? You might be surprised at how different your daily life is when your online life is less involved. Social media influences us in ways we may not realize. We are always comparing our body to other people in photos and we may have FOMO if we see people we know out having fun. FOMO is the Fear Of Missing Out. Social media is well-known for making people feel FOMO all the time.

Day #10: Say No & Don't Feel Guilty

Say no to something today. Or, if there is something in your life you've been going along with but actually do not enjoy or are no longer comfortable with, say no to this thing today. Decide to do what is right for you. And, when you finally do, don't feel guilty for it. You are allowed to make positive choices for yourself. If someone has a negative reaction to you saying no, take this as a good thing. This is a great opportunity for you to try your boundary setting skills. And, if they still do not respect your wishes even after you set a boundary around "saying no" then this may not be a person you want around, especially during your journey to overcome IS.

Day #11: Stop An Activity You Don't Enjoy

Along the same lines of "saying no," stop doing something you don't enjoy. This could be hanging out with a certain person, going to a certain restaurant, or even working a job you don't like. This is your life! If you are engaging in activities that do not fulfill you and cultivate happiness, then it will be difficult for you to feel confident in yourself. When we keep doing things we don't like, we forget about the things we do like. Our passions are deeply rooted in our sense of self. Furthermore, they are further rooted in our purpose in life.

We can all find our purpose through the things we truly enjoy. When we stop doing these things, we lose our passion, and it's a terrible cycle.

Day #12: Forgive, But Don't Forget

We have all been wronged before. In some situations, we cannot let the person back into our life. This is a day when you can mentally forgive this person or persons. But, we don't want to forget this. Do not let this person back into your personal life and safe space. Doing so could jeopardize your confidence and peace. Allow yourself to cut out negativity whether in the form of a person or activity. Also allow yourself to forgive! This creates a stronger inner peace and healthier life. You do not have to reach out to this person and say: "I forgive you!" This forgiveness is about *you*. It's not selfish to decide to let something go when it hurts you. Forgiving the person and the situation frees you from its negative grasp on you.

Day #13: Feel Good About Yourself

There's plenty of ways to cultivate good feelings. What makes you feel good? What do you like to do? Do one of a few of these today. Maybe you want to treat yourself to your favorite food, or get your hair done, or go for a hike. Life is about working hard, but it also meant to be enjoyed. If we can't enjoy our life, then we won't work as hard. There has to be joy at the foundation of all we do. While there will not always be happy times, we should keep in mind the importance of feeling good about ourselves.

Day #14: Take a Break

What do you need a break from? It could be from work, family, from our partner, etc. We all need to take a sick day every now and then! And, we all need time alone from the people we love. It doesn't mean we love them any less, but just that we need some time for ourselves. When you're taking this break, you can do something that makes you feel good. Take a note from the day before and engage in an activity you truly enjoy. This will ensure you are rested and ready to take on any coming obstacle.

Day #15: Surround Yourself With Good People

Only keep the people who lift you up around. If you currently have people in your life who tear you down at every opportunity and just make you feel bad, do not keep them around you. You won't be able to build inner confidence when there are people outside of you who are working to take that confidence away. Surrounding yourself with good people will help you on those tough days when you are struggling to keep your confidence up. They will remind you of your true self and be there to pick you back up.

Day #16: Be Mindful of Your Diet

The food we eat can influence our mindset. If we always have junk food, then our body has to process this and all the chemicals can affect the way we think. Eating healthy foods will keep our body physically healthy and our minds sharp. This alone can keep us confident. If we feed our body unhealthy food and we have a lack of the nutrients we need, then we will not function at our best. Food is something we all need to survive, and making healthy choices could improve your situation immediately.

Day #17: End Relationships that Don't Support You

Throughout this book, we have talked about the importance of finding strength from within. But, we have also touched on how the influences around us can be damaging. If there are still people in your life who do not support you in any way, really ask yourself what the benefit of keeping them in your life is. Would they be there for you if you really needed them? Would you be there for them? Many people with IS go above and beyond for other people, but may not get the same in return. If you recognize a relationship like this in your life, make a decision today to either end it or confront the other party about their behavior toward you.

Day #18: Create Boundaries

This is the day where you can begin creating boundaries if you have not done this yet. Take it slow and make a promise to yourself to set one boundary today. It could be something small, like deciding that you will not sacrifice your Friday evening for work like you normally would or saying no to that toxic family member. You can use this step if you say no on Day #15 and still feel guilty about it. Taking the step to create a boundary will give you the confidence of sticking up for yourself! And, it will show you that you truly do know what is right for you.

Day #19: Be Alone

Being alone is difficult for those with imposter feelings. Sometimes it opens the gates for those negative feelings to come in. But, in order to be a healthy individual, alone time is a crucial step for personal growth. We all need time to reset and be alone with ourselves. We are the ones stuck in our mind all the time. We may as well learn how to be with ourselves and let distractions fall to the side just for this day. When you can be with your inner self and not afraid, your confidence will naturally increase. You can feel assured that no matter what goes on outside of yourself, you will be okay with your inner life.

Day #20: Find a Purpose

Finding a purpose, whether big or small, will give you the confidence of striving toward something. It feels good to know *why* you are taking action! You may not be sure right this moment what your purpose is, and that's okay. Our purpose can change and take different forms throughout life. But, each day, try to find some purpose as you go throughout your routine. This is why it's so crucial to do the previous steps and engage in exciting activities, take breaks, and make yourself feel good. It is through all of these things we can discover our passion. Often, our passion is unexpected. It may be rooted in a natural skill or something completely outside our realm of usual engagements.

Day #21: Gratitude vs. Problems

Life can be difficult. But, when you are able to, focus on the things you are grateful for. It's actually easier to get lost in all the problems you may have. At the end of the night, you may lay awake in bed listing all of your worries. It's harder to focus on what's going right because it's already good. We don't want to ignore these things either, because they may pass before we have a chance to take them in fully and be grateful for them. Much like finding a purpose each day, you can also find something you are grateful for each day no matter how small. Shifting our focus to the things we are grateful for can decrease our stress and even help attract better things in the future.

Day 22: Work On Your Anxiety

Anxiety often comes alone with imposter feelings. We can be overwhelmed by them, and the stress takes over our life, clouding even the most positive aspects. People work on their anxiety in all different ways. Find the best way for yourself. Anxiety is different for everyone. For some people, therapy is a great tool. Others find exercise useful. But, if you find that your anxiety is becoming too much, it is definitely time to talk to a professional. They may be able to help get to the root of your problems and even prescribe medication if it is the right thing for you. Many of us struggle with anxiety and just try to deal with it alone. But, it can compound the imposter feelings. If we work on this anxiety, it will give us the confidence we need to work on other things. This is all part of the process to a healthier life.

Day #23: Don't Take It Personally

Everyone is going about their life just as you are. We are all doing the best we can. We can't escape our own mind, which means we carry our struggles everywhere we go. Think of how many people you see each day. Each person you see is dealing with someone unique. They may take out their frustration on you. Maybe your boss snapped at you over something small, or a lady in the grocery store gave you a dirty look. We often take these moments throughout our day too personally. Take every event like this with a grain of salt. Ask yourself: What is going on in that person's life that is causing them to act this way? And, what is going on in mine that they may not know about? Have I ever lashed out at someone who didn't deserve it? People have a tendency to do this to their loved ones, because they know instinctively that their loved ones will never leave them. Be conscious of what others are going through as well as your own attitude.

Day #24: Be Your Own Person Before Loving Others

Many people will look for a relationship in order to feel whole. This is actually setting them up for failure. You should be a whole, confident person on your own. You want to be your best version before entering into a partnership with anyone else. We can't possibly bring our best self to the table if we are not whole on our own. If you are expecting your partner to "fix" you or help you through internal struggles, it will create an unhealthy dynamic. While two people in a relationship can become extremely close, no one is a mind reader. No partner should have to sacrifice themselves in order to make another whole. If you are unsure about being whole by yourself, then it means you should spend more time searching for what you want and need in your life. This should always be a priority. And, it does not make you selfish! It is a sign of health and maturity to work on yourself first.

Day #25: Allow for the Right Timing

When we are working toward something, we often want the result immediately. But everything takes time. This day connects with Day #8! Accept where you are now. It is a reminder that although you may want to be somewhere else, you are here right now. We might have an idea of exactly *how* and *when* something should happen, but this is just not how it works! I sure wish it was. We have to trust in the timing of our life. When we do this, it's surprising how much may happen. We talked about the benefits of relinquishing control and how freeing it can be. Try this here! Let go of the need to control the timing in your life. We will never know what great things can happen when we let them!

Day #26: Understand Everyone Has Different Talents

When we see other people doing well in one area that we are not doing well in, those imposter feelings can try to convince us that it means we are no longer good enough. This could not be farther from the truth. We are all born with intrinsic talents. And, we can cultivate new ones throughout our life. Just because someone else is beautiful, or talented, or smart, does not mean you aren't! Remember your talents in these moments of insecurity. It's good to write them down and read them aloud when you forget. We all need reminders of who we are. I know for sure that I can be my harshest critic. People with IS take this to another level and may compare their worst selves to the best version of another person.

Day #27: Love Your Body!

Many people with IS also struggle with body image issues. It's hard to simply say, "Love Your Body!" because we all know it's not that easy. It's a long process to get comfortable with yourself. But, just for today, allow yourself a break. Love your body today. Do something you love. Move it in a way you like. This could be going for a bike ride, walking, or sitting on the couch! Eat some of your favorite foods. Our body is what carries us through. Be kind to it and nourish it today. Our body can be an ongoing process too! Maybe you have gained some weight and are looking to lose it. That's great! The opportunity to make a change should be looked at as a challenge. Remind yourself that you are always a work in progress. We all are!

Day #28: Listen to Music!

Music has a special healing power. Whatever your favorite kind of music is, blast it today! It has the ability to pull us out of bad moods, move us to emotion, and connect us to our inner selves. *Have you ever been riding in the car and that perfect song comes on the radio?* It completely changes your mood and you find yourself rocking along to it your whole ride. Music brings dopamine to the brain. This is a chemical which is associated with pleasure and reward! So, much like exercise, music brings healthy chemicals that can alter your mood.

Day #29: Visualize Good Things for Yourself

When we think positively, we encourage positivity in our life. Regardless of how negative certain aspects of your life are at this moment, look to the future with anticipation. Imagine the things you want. Write them down. Talk about them as if they have already happened! Become so sure about the new trajectory of your life that soon enough you will get there. If you are certain enough that these things will happen, you will begin doing things consciously and subconsciously to get yourself to that destination! A negative attitude will keep you at a standstill. Visualizing and focusing on what you want can change your life sooner.

Day #30: Acknowledge Your Strength

Even if you don't feel it, you are strong. You have decided to make a change in your life! The imposter syndrome can really knock us down. But, you have fought it this long and have the confidence to make a good change for yourself. Hopefully by Day #30, your confidence has increased! You have learned how to do what is right for you! Putting yourself first when you need to heal is never a sign of selfishness, but is instead a clear sign of personal strength.

Why You Deserve Happiness

Have you ever thought along this journey: *Well, what if I just don't deserve happiness?* You may not even want to try any of these steps because you have a nagging feeling that you just don't deserve to change. You have stayed in this way of thinking for so long and have found comfort in it. I am here to tell you that this simply is not true. We all deserve happiness. There are a million things in life that can hold us back from feeling this same happiness, but at the end of the day, we all deserve it. Maybe you have found that you subconsciously won't allow yourself to be happy or the situations and people around you are preventing that happiness from coming to its full form.

There is a phrase I hear often: "I wasn't meant to do (blank)." This is a phrase I don't agree with. While we all have our passions, we can put in the hard work and set our mind to do anything. None of us really know what we are *meant to be* or *meant to do*. The only being who knows that is whatever greater spirit is out there. But, we can have the self-awareness to see the things we are passionate about and the things that make us feel something, giving us the confidence to live the life we want. We can then take the knowledge of what those passions are and truly discover what we are meant to be. This is where our dreams come from! We discover our passion for sports and want to go professional or we love to write poetry and make a goal to publish some of our poems.

This is why our reason for doing anything and the intention behind it is so important. If we have the right reason and put in the work, it will eventually come to fruition. Maybe you have always wanted to be a singer but won't take the time to record music and post it online. There is no way you will reach this goal if you don't put in the work! It's great you know what your passion is and have a goal for it, but without the time, it will never happen. Another example could be that you want to become a marathon runner, but only because you want to tell people you won the gold medal. The reasoning behind your goal is not a positive one and it probably will not carry you all the way. You have to do it for you!

So, let's say you're ready to put in the hard work and you have the right reason behind it. But, *you still feel like you don't deserve to do it.* Our beliefs come from somewhere! They come from our childhood and past experiences we have already lived through. Maybe a relationship you really cared about failed and you took on the blame. Or, maybe you were always told that you were not worthy as a child and the blame in the household was all put on you.

Regardless of where you got this belief from, it is completely wrong! Let me say this again: *You are worthy and deserve happiness!* But, somewhere along the way, you went along with this false belief that you don't deserve happiness. And, it's now preventing you from moving forward in your life. In a way, it allows you a free pass. You may think, "Well, I don't deserve this anyway, so I won't even try." So, you don't try! And you stay stuck in this negative thought cycle of wanting to change, but convincing yourself it's better not to try.

It's time to change this narrative with the truth. Only you can realize that you are worthy, and be the one who is willing to put in the work! Repeat it over and over if you have to. "I am worthy. I am worthy!" Set a reminder in your phone. Write it on your mirror in the bathroom. Whatever you do, don't forget the truth. We all have the power to control our mindset and ground our beliefs in reality. And the reality is: You deserve to live the life you've always wanted.

Chapter Summary

In this final chapter, we talked about the range of things that may get in the way of dealing with your insecurities. We all need the confidence to fight against them. It's good to distinguish between confidence and ego, because they are completely different. Finally, we discussed your 30-Day confidence challenge and how you can get back to your most healthy and confident self.

Final Words

Dealing with imposter syndrome every day can leave you exhausted and confused. You are always doubting your abilities, feeling like a phony, and doing everything you can to reach up to your expectations but still feeling like you are not enough. You feel like everyone around you knows you're a fake, and any moment now someone will call you out for it. Hopefully, you took the Clance IP test in the first chapter. Maybe you found that you have moderate characteristics, or maybe you discovered that you have intense characteristics of IS.

Thankfully, we all have the ability to stop feeling like a fraud and rebuild our confidence. No matter how loud that inner critic gets, we can silence it with positivity. It is within every one of us to take back control of our awareness and break this pattern of thinking.

Sadly, there is no one cause for these imposter feelings! We did talk about the various possibilities. It can be a variety of reasons and often it is not only one cause. However, it seems for most sufferers, that the reason stems back to childhood. Many children faced high expectations or may have lived in an abusive home. They grow up to set these same expectations in their adult life. Or, they are used to performing in order to impress others. In some cases, you may not have felt those IS feelings until your adulthood! We know that major life changes can cause initial feelings of IS. The most sinister aspect of this cause is that these life changes can be good! You may have been accepted into a well-known graduate program or finally received that promotion. But, now you feel like you don't deserve it.

Everyone experiences IS differently. But there are five common types discovered by Dr. Valerie Young, an expert on imposter syndrome. These types follow the most common symptoms closely. The five common types: The Perfectionist, The Superwoman/man, The Natural genius, The Expert, and The Soloist. Each type is unique in the way imposter feelings measure the person's worth.

For the perfectionist, overcoming their need for everything to be right includes unlearning negative habits of thinking. They measure their worth on things being done 100% correct. 99% does not make the cut! Not everything will always be 100%, but imposter feelings will try to tell us that it is because we are not good enough when it is simply because we are human! For perfectionists, a heavy focus on realistic thinking can ground you in reality when those imposter thoughts take over.

This need for everything to be right can connect to the imposter workaholic! You may overwork yourself in order to prove your worth. This is because the superwoman/man type measures their worth on outside validation.. When we are constantly looking for validation from the outside, we cultivate a negative self-esteem. You may work all hours of the night, constantly put in over 40 hours a week at work, and still feel like you are not good enough. Finding the awareness to look inside and validate who we are in this moment is how we can overcome this inability to relax and stop working.

As humans, we will not know everything. No matter how many degrees and certifications we receive, knowing everything is not something we can do. But, you might be so afraid of being discovered as unknowledgeable that you join the expert type of IS. This type measures themself based on how much knowledge they accumulate. We talked about a fear of not being good enough and where this comes from. Learning to feel good enough about ourselves is the key to overcoming this fear. We also have to surrender! It's so freeing to allow ourselves to realize that we don't know everything.

With any change, it will take time. The natural genius may struggle with this a bit, as they measure their worth on how quickly they can accomplish a goal. Don't let this need to succeed hold you back from trying new things! Embrace learning and embrace this process. Admitting you don't know everything will allow others in your life to help!

The soloist may struggle with this particular step as asking for help is outside their comfort zone. They measure their worth in how much they can accomplish by themselves. For all people struggling with imposter syndrome, remember, it does not make you weak to ask for help! We are social creatures and rely on our connections with each other to get through life. Facing your fears will only allow a greater opportunity for you and those around you to achieve.

You are now armed against imposter syndrome with your 30-Day Confidence Challenge! In the final chapter, we went day by day through steps that will help quiet your inner critic and bring you back to your truest self. The reasons to move forward through your insecurities are endless. But only you know why you want to make this change and the steps that will work for you. Whatever type you fall into and however IS manifests in your life, don't forget that you can fight back against it and change the path you are currently on. Everyone deserves happiness and a life where they feel fulfilled. Accept your accomplishments and remember to focus on where you want to be in the future, all with an acceptance and appreciation of where you are now.

"4 Reasons You Grew Up Feeling Not Good Enough." *Psych Central*, 2 Apr. 2018, https://psychcentral.com/blog/psychology-self/2018/04/not-good-enough.

"5 Types of Imposter Syndrome and How to Stop Them." *The Muse*, https://www.themuse.com/advice/5-different-types-of-imposter-syndrome-and-5-ways-to-battle-each-one. Accessed 13 June 2021.

"5 Ways Smart People Sabotage Their Success." *Harvard Business Review*, Nov. 2018. *hbr.org*, https://hbr.org/2018/11/5-ways-smart-people-sabotage-their-success.

"8 Reasons to Overcome Your Fear of Asking for Help." *ms focus Magazine*, https://www.msfocusmagazine.org/Magazine/Magazine-Items/Posted/8-Reasons-to-Overcome-Your-Fear-of-Asking-for-Help. Accessed 13 June 2021.

"10 Things to Do When You Think You're Not Good Enough." *Lifehack*, 15 May 2019, https://www.lifehack.org/833075/not-feeling-good-enough.

"13 Ways To Stop Seeking The Approval Of Others & Feel Super Confident." *Bustle*, https://www.bustle.com/articles/159055-13-ways-to-stop-seeking-the-approval-of-others-feel-super-confident. Accessed 13 June 2021.

"17 Ways to Validate Yourself." *Live Well with Sharon Martin*, 20 Dec. 2019, https://www.livewellwithsharonmartin.com/validate-yourself/.

"30 Ways To Practice Self-Love And Be Good To Yourself." *Lifehack*, 12 Aug. 2014, https://www.lifehack.org/articles/communication/30-ways-practice-self-love-and-good-yourself.html.

breathe. "A Roadmap to Overcoming Insecurities." *Zen Habits*, 14 Mar. 2016, https://zenhabits.net/insecurities/.

Council, Forbes Coaches. "Council Post: 13 Tips For Overcoming Your Fear Of Asking For Help." *Forbes*, https://www.forbes.com/sites/forbescoachescouncil/2018/12/11/13-tips-for-overcoming-your-fear-of-asking-for-help/. Accessed 13 June 2021.

Definition of SYNDROME. https://www.merriam-webster.com/dictionary/syndrome. Accessed 13 June 2021.

"Do You Have a Codependent Personality? | Everyday Health." *EverydayHealth.Com*, https://www.everydayhealth.com/emotional-health/do-you-have-a-codependent-personality.aspx. Accessed 13 June 2021.

Dr. Pauline Rose Clance - IMPOSTOR PHENOMENON. https://www.paulineroseclance.com/impostor_phenomenon.html. Accessed 13 June 2021.

Forbes, https://www.forbes.com/sites/cywakeman/2015/11/23/confidence-vs-ego-the-difference-between-success-and-self-sabotage/. Accessed 13 June 2021.

H, Steven and el. "Don't Be Afraid to Ask For Help: It's a Strength, Not a Weakness." *The Emotion Machine*, 22 Feb. 2013, https://www.theemotionmachine.com/dont-be-afraid-to-ask-for-help/.

"How to Stop Feeling Like an Outsider When You Have Social Anxiety." *Verywell Mind,* https://www.verywellmind.com/imposter-syndrome-and-social-anxiety-disorder-4156469. Accessed 13 June 2021.

"Imposter Syndrome: What It Is & How to Overcome It." *Healthline,* 16 Apr. 2021, https://www.healthline.com/health/mental-health/imposter-syndrome.

Imposter Syndrome: Why You Have It and What You Can Do About It. https://zapier.com/blog/what-is-imposter-syndrome/. Accessed 13 June 2021.

"Making Sense of Character Strengths." *Verywell Mind,* https://www.verywellmind.com/what-are-character-strengths-4843090. Accessed 13 June 2021.

Morgan, Nozomi, et al. "5 Ways to Conquer Fear and Ask for Help." *HuffPost,* 5 Nov. 2015, https://www.huffpost.com/entry/5-ways-to-conquer-fear-an_b_8479562.

says, How to make ANYONE love you {PROVEN}-COUCHING BLOG. "7 Proven Strategies to Stop Being a Know-It-All." *Alli Polin | Break The Frame,* 9 June 2015, https://breaktheframe.com/stop-being-a-know-it-all/.

"The Critical Inner Voice Explained." *PsychAlive,* 18 June 2009, https://www.psychalive.org/critical-inner-voice/.

"The Strength of Surrender." *Project Happiness,* https://shop.projecthappiness.org/blogs/project-happiness/the-strength-of-surrender. Accessed 13 June 2021.

"The Science Behind Why Music Makes Us Feel So Good." *Lifehack*, 9 Feb. 2016, https://www.lifehack.org/361240/the-science-behind-why-music-makes-feel-good.

"Want To Look Competent? Ask For Advice." *Time*, https://time.com/3158889/ask-for-advice-competent/. Accessed 13 June 2021.Wakeman, Cy. "Confidence Vs. Ego: The Difference Between Success And Self-Sabotage."

What Is Splitting Psychology? | Betterhelp. https://www.betterhelp.com/advice/psychologists/what-is-splitting-psychology/. Accessed 13 June 2021.

"Why Your Boundaries Matter Now More Than Ever." *CBT Psychology*, 28 Aug. 2020, http://cbtpsychology.com/relational-boundaries/.

Why You Deserve Success, Happiness And Fulfillment Just As Much As Anyone Else - T. Harv Eker. https://www.harveker.com/deserve-success-happiness-fulfillment-just-much-anyone-else/. Accessed 13 June 2021.

"Why Your Whole Self Feels Ashamed But Only Part of You Feels Guilty." *Verywell Mind*, https://www.verywellmind.com/what-is-shame-425328. Accessed 13 June 2021.

"Your 30 Day Confidence Challenge: Put Yourself Outside Of Your Comfort Zone And Find Your Inner Strength." *Thought Catalog*, 5 Oct. 2018, https://thoughtcatalog.com/leena-lomeli/2018/10/your-30-day-confidence-challenge-put-yourself-outside-of-your-comfort-zone-and-find-your-inner-strength/.